The Seven Deadly Sins

The Seven

Angus Wilson
Edith Sitwell
Cyril Connolly
Patrick Leigh Fermor
Evelyn Waugh
Christopher Sykes
W. H. Auden

Special Foreword by IAN FLEMING

Introduction by RAYMOND MORTIMER

WILLIAM MORROW AND COMPANY
NEW YORK

Deadly Sins

WILLIAM MORROW AND COMPANY
NEW YORK

PRINTED AND BOUND IN GREAT BRITAIN
by W. S. Cowell Ltd, Butter Market, Ipswich

Contents

A Note on the Illustrations

The title page illustration is from a South German woodcut of 1414 and illustrates 'The World' – personification of the Seven Deadly Sins. The figure offers a cup representing gluttony. Her diadem represents pride; the bodice – lust; the severed left hand – sloth; the belt – covetousness; the wolf's head (to the left) – anger, and the dog's head – envy. The significance of the rest of the body is that the right leg represents life and the left leg with the snake's head – death.

The illustrations used with each of the essays come from a coloured woodcut, all in one piece, entitled 'The Seven Deadly Sins and the Devil' now in the Albertina Collection, Vienna. It is dated 1480–90 and originates in the district of Constance.

Foreword

I HAVE various qualifications for writing an introduction to this series of distinguished and highly
entertaining essays.

First of all, I invented the idea of the series
when, a couple of years ago, I was still a member
of the Editorial Board of the London *Sunday Times*.
This Board meets every Tuesday to comment on the
issue of the previous Sunday, discuss the plans for the
next issue and put forward longer-term projects.

It is quite a small Board of seven or eight heads of
departments – I was Foreign Manager at the time –
together with the Editor and the Proprietor, Mr Roy
Thomson, and we are all good friends, though at this
weekly meeting, beneath the surface of our friendliness,
lurk all the deadly sins with the exception of gluttony
and lust. Each one of us has pride in our department of
the paper; many of us are covetous of the editorial
chair; most are envious of the bright ideas put forward
by others; anger comes to the surface at what we regard
as unmerited criticism, and sloth, certainly in my case,
lurks in the wings.

The same pattern is probably followed at all execu-
tive meetings in all branches of business. When someone
else puts up a bright idea, however useful or profitable
it may be to the business concerned, traces at least of

Envy, Anger and Covetousness will be roused in his colleagues. Yet, on the occasion when I put forward this particular 'bright' idea for the future, I seem to remember nothing but approbation and a genial nodding of heads.

The project was outside my own sphere of action on the paper and I heard nothing more of it until I had left the *Sunday Times* to concentrate on writing thrillers centred round a member of the British Secret Service called James Bond. So I cannot describe what troubles the Literary Editor ran into in his endeavours to marry the Seven Deadly Sins to seven appropriate authors. So far as I can recall, the marriages I myself had suggested were closely followed, except that I had suggested Mr Malcolm Muggeridge to write on the theme of Anger on the grounds that he is such an extremely angry man. In the event, as you will see, Mr W. H. Auden was the brilliant choice.

My next claim to introduce these essays was my suggestion to Mr Lawrence Hughes, a friend of mine and a Director of William Morrow & Co., that he should publish them in a book. Usually when one makes brilliant suggestions to a publisher, a dull glaze comes over his eyes and nothing happens. But in this case Larry Hughes was enthusiastic and, despite all kinds of copyright problems, energetically pursued my suggestion and gathered these seven famous English authors together between hard covers – no mean feat if you know anything about copyright and literary agents.

So you might think I could justifiably allow myself a modest indulgence in the deadly sin of Pride. You would be mistaken. I have read and re-read these essays with pleasure and profit, but their moral impact upon me has been uncomfortable. To be precise and truthful, the critical examination of these famous sins by some of the keenest brains of today has led me to the dreadful conclusion that in fact all these ancient sins, compared with the sins of today, are in fact very close to virtues.

To run through the list. I have always admired the Pride of Dame Edith Sitwell, the pride which, with her proudful brothers, has carried this remarkable literary family through battles of opinion and taste reaching back to my youth.

The Covetousness of Cyril Connolly, which he takes off so brilliantly in his piece of fiction, is one of his most endearing qualities and he would be a smaller and less interesting man without it.

The Gluttony for life, food, drink and women of Patrick Leigh-Fermor are the essence of his tremendous zest for everything. Lust? If Christopher Sykes is lustful, may he, and I for the matter of that, long remain so.

Envy has its ugly sides, but if I, as a second son amongst four, had not been envious of my elder brother and his achievements I would not have wished all my life to try and emulate him. As for Anger, surely we all need more rather than less of it to combat the indifference, the 'I'm all right, Jack' attitudes, of today.

Of all the seven, only Sloth in its extreme form of *accidia*, which is a form of spiritual suicide and a refusal of joy, so brilliantly examined by Evelyn Waugh, has my wholehearted condemnation, perhaps because in moments of despair I have seen its face.

How drab and empty life would be without these sins, and what dull dogs we all would be without a healthy trace of many of them in our make up! And has not the depiction of these sins and their consequences been the yeast in most great fiction and drama? Could Shakespeare, Voltaire, Balzac, Dostoevsky or Tolstoy have written their masterpieces if humanity had been innocent of these sins? It is almost as if Leonardo, Titian, Rembrandt and Van Gogh had been required to paint without using the primary colours.

The truth, of course, is that generally speaking these Seven Deadly Sins were enumerated by monks for monks, and one can easily see how mischievous and harmful they could be within a monastery.

We do not live in a monastery, but in a great pulsating ant heap, and this brings me back to the moral confusion into which I have been thrown by these essays and which amounts to feeling that there are other and deadlier sins which I would like to see examined by authors of equal calibre in a companion volume to this.

I have made a list of these Seven Deadlier Sins which every reader will no doubt wish to amend, and these are my seven: Avarice, Cruelty, Snobbery, Hypocrisy, Self-righteousness, Moral Cowardice and Malice. If I were to put these modern seven into the scales against the ancient seven I cannot but feel that the weight of the former would bring the brass tray crashing down.

But is this loose thinking? Could it perhaps be argued that if we are free of the ancient seven we shall not fall victim to their modern progeny? I personally do not think so, but it would need better brains than mine and a keener sense of theological morality than I possess to pursue the argument. As a man in the street, I can only express my belief that being possessed of the ancient seven deadly sins one can still go to heaven, whereas to be afflicted by the modern variations can only be a passport to hell.

And by the same token, what about the Seven Deadly Virtues?

What about the anal-eroticism which the psychologists tell us lies at the base of Frugality? How much is Charity worth when it springs from self-interest? Is political acumen a virtue as practised by the Communists? What hell Sociability can be! Where is the line to be drawn between Deference and, not to use a more vulgar, hyphenated word, Sycophancy? Neatness in excess becomes pathological, so does Cleanliness. How often is Chastity a cloak for frigidity?

But I have held you for too long from these wonderful, and each in its different way exciting, essays and I must at all costs avoid that deadliest of all sins, ancient or modern, a sin which is surely more durable than any of those I have enumerated – that of being a Bore.

Introduction

by Raymond Mortimer

PRIDE, Covetousness, Gluttony, Lust, Sloth, Envy, Anger – those are the sins considered deadly by St Thomas Aquinas and by Western Churchmen ever since. As they are sins, not crimes, we have to seek light on them from the only experts upon the matter, the theologians. In any case the selection seems curious, and to explain it we must go far back into ecclesiastical history.

The earliest enumeration contained eight sins. In the early fifth century, Cassian, for instance, who introduced to the West the rules of Eastern monasticism, included vainglory as well as pride, dejection as well as sloth or *accidia*, and did not mention envy. His treatise dealt with the sins as the chief obstacles to perfection in monks. They were soon reduced to seven, a number that had long enjoyed particular prestige.

The deadly (or capital) sins (or vices) are distinguished not by their gravity but by their power of generating other sins. We might untheologically describe them as evil states of mind that tempt men into a variety of evil acts; covetousness can obviously lead to burglary or blackmail, anger to murder or arson, sloth to despair and suicide. States of mind such as heresy and lack of faith are mortal sins, which the seven in themselves can seldom be.

Since the Middle Ages, and especially during the past hundred years, there has been a continuous change in ethical values. As the Catholic Encyclopaedia puts it, 'Evolution has revolutionized morality, sin is no more.' The rationalist has replaced the notion of sin, which is an offence against God, by the notion of wrong, which is an offence against one's neighbour or oneself. The effects of this change are apparent even among orthodox believers in sin. Slave-owning, for instance, although not in itself a sin, would certainly be discouraged by moral theologians; and cruelty to animals (again not sinful) is thought wrong by Christians, at any rate in Northern countries.

In a series of articles such as I am introducing, passionate denunciation and threats of brimstone would be out of place. Moreover, the contributors have naturally concentrated upon the particular sin each is discussing without much reference to the grave offences that this may produce. Even so, the mildness with which on the whole they regard the deadly sins may be thought surprising and significant. We have come a long way from the thirteenth century, when St Thomas enlarged upon the hideous power of the Deadly Seven, and even from the nineteenth, when horror of sin was impressed upon children as soon as they could walk.

At least three of the contributors are known to be orthodox Christians; yet one who is not has written the only piece that makes a sin nauseous and terrifying. By satire without invective Mr Connolly shows how covetousness can corrupt a man into a monster of egotism. How temperate by comparison the Christian author who deals with sloth! This English word does not carry the full sense of the Latin *accidia*, which means spiritual torpor and refusal of joy, or, as a modern Jesuit has put it, 'the don't care feeling'. This was a sin that specially beset the monk or nun who lacked a vocation – a type common in the Middle Ages. Mr Evelyn Waugh finds a modern parallel in the 'browned off' soldier. But the allied sin of *pigritia* (which he translates as 'plain slackness') has become, he points out, far more usual and now endangers our civilization as well as our morality.

Anger is defined by theologians as the desire for vengeance; and Mr Auden here accordingly condemns most official punishment of crime as retributive instead of deterrent or remedial. In this country, he also observes, the middle classes are trained to display their anger not in physical aggression but in verbal malice. Theologians would presumably agree that uncharitable talk is a sin that often besets even those who can resist the grosser temptations.

Mr Angus Wilson presents envy as an affliction rather than a sin, and invites our pity for those who suffer from it – notably writers, who in his opinion (not in mine) are prone to it as an occupational malady. The educational ladder – now so strangely denounced as a 'rat-race' – has multiplied, he believes, the incidence of envy. Anti-Americanism exhibits upon a national scale this most unenjoyable of sins.

Gluttony could doubtless become obsessive in a monk confined to a meagre and most unappetising diet; but, even so, I should have thought it would expend itself in daydreams rather than generate other sins. Perhaps it maintains its place among the Deadly Seven because it covers excessive indulgence in drink as well as in food, and drunkenness may unleash a variety of vices. Gluttony in the secular sense of the word may damage

the sinner's health but rarely harms his neighbours. It seems comical rather than wicked, and has accordingly inspired Mr Leigh-Fermor to dazzle us with a firework display of erudition and wit.

The Christian case against lust is expounded admirably. Mr Sykes suggests, however, that this sin may have been given undue prominence by ecclesiastics: Christ was far more severe in the Gospels upon hypocrisy, hardness of heart and the respectability of the conventionally religious. Pride, the chief of the Deadly Sins according to Saints Gregory and Thomas, gets off lightly at the hands of another Christian. Dame Edith Sitwell has 'never regarded it, except in certain cases, as a major sin,' and although she cites Iago as a supreme example of wicked pride, does not pay even lip-service to humility, offering examples only of its ugliness.

These articles have fascinated me, and I should like to read the same writers upon other forms of wickedness – Mr Waugh, for example on cowardice, Mr Wilson on hypocrisy, Mr Auden on racial prejudice, Mr Sykes on uncharitableness, Mr Leigh-Fermor on mischief-making and Dame Edith on cruelty to animals. I can imagine no more telling proof of the change in our moral values, for would not the repugnance displayed be remarkably more violent?

ENVY

ENVY

Angus Wilson

WITH some it is said to begin in the cradle. The milk they suck turns sour on them as they think of the richer draught on which the infant earl is feeding up at the hall. To discern this is, no doubt, one of the painful intuitive powers of a mother. At least these underprivileged infants must be free from the hideous extra distortion of smiling, of putting on a brave front, demanded by society of the envious in their adult years.

These babies are, in any case, infant prodigies. The first twist of Envy in the guts comes for most people over a decade later. Perhaps on that proud occasion when they first see their name in print in the local or even national newspaper; or more humbly, but no less devastatingly, in a long typewritten list set off against a background of green baize.

As examinations increasingly determine the irrevocable status of human beings, come, that is, to shape the second or social self which a man must carry around with him for the rest of his life, these first stabs of Envy will no doubt strike more people, and earlier and more cruelly.

But that momentary sick green pallor which, at the sight of the rival's name set above his own, robs the schoolboy's (or schoolgirl's) face of its natural healthy glow does not, of course, mean that he will become an addict to the pleasure-pains of Envy. That emotion, like its twin, jealousy, is after all abnormally in evidence in our schooldays; it is then that the competitive spirit, fostered by the closed hot-house atmosphere, twists and twines its liana grip round the lives of the young – a bracing preparation, it is said, for the jungle world to come.

Yet even among these young envious there are some who will never be free from the pains again. How can one distinguish these, so damned at that early age? Probably by the way in which they meet the school's other little preparation for the jungle to come – the demand that they shall lose with a good face.

Saved the boy (or girl) who can show enough annoyance to give vent to his feelings, even allow himself an open expression of regret at the success of his particular rival, and then pass on quickly (but not too quickly) to the next business of the day. Damned, of course, the boy who slinks off with twisted face and slouching gait, or the girl who bursts into tears of rage.

Twice damned the boy who tries with an affectedly adult drawl to express his contempt for the exam, his surprise that anyone should have expected him to do any better or his rival less well. Twice damned the girl who now suggests that boys or dress had taken up all her preparation time. Too late for such sophisticated excuses. Not to have worked hard in preparation for examinations appears an elegance only in the successful.

Yet there is worse than this. Thrice damned the wretched creature who rushes off to mingle with the congratulatory knot clustered round the winner, who feels it incumbent as the loser to make the presentation speech at the celebration party. *Her* face will wear that painful grimace of sour good loserliness again and again in her coming life, until at last she is never quite parted from it: in constant expectation of the next stroke of good luck - that will come of course to her neighbour but never to her. *His* voice will take on more and more the envious friend's strange hearty tones that somehow come out as a snarl, that jolly laugh that always turns into a snakelike hiss before it has died away in the air.

As in those awful post-exam days their rival's name seems to be on the whole school's lips, so in the future there will always be one name, among all the many that they envy, which will haunt and taunt them where-ever they go. On 'bad days' - for the chronic enviers have their bilious, black 'bad days' - that rival's name will seem to stare from every poster and be carried on the wind from the conversation of every chance passer-by. Envy will by then have become their overriding emo-tion, a secret shame to hide and to hug, a poisonous, habit-forming drug they cannot live without, and must die from at last.

What drives a man first into this hopeless pantomime of pretended ease and insouciant losing? Not chiefly, I think, social opinion, the continued voice of the school demanding from him a show of good sportsmanship. Much more, I suspect, the secret sly pressure of those already addicted to Envy. Any contorted grimace in-tended to mimic happiness is worth attempting – if it can hide us from the searching eye of other envious men, who seek by their commiseration to enlist us to their lost brotherhood.

Yet just as, with wrenching effort, you bring yourself to utter that friendly carefree 'Jolly good' or 'Well done' to the man who has taken the prize from you, the lurking Envy addict catches your eye, lets you know that for him at least your words did not ring true. The 'happy act' must be of a high standard if it is to deceive him.

Once recruited to the mysteries of the envious, com-mitted to the little cruel digs of false comfort by which they communicate with one another, only a miracle or a stroke of good luck can release you. If you could arrange for a complete stranger to leave his fortune to you; or persuade some lunatic chairman of an enterprise with which you have no connection to offer you a well-paid sinecure on the board; if, with no preliminary ado on your part, the most beautiful and popular girl in your circle should fall for you madly; if by some freakish change of the wind you could yourself become Adonis over-night - then you could be released from the iron circle of Envy which slowly but surely is narrowing and strangling your life.

But then you would have had 'good luck', and, by their very definition of themselves the envious never have 'good luck'; that is the property of those whom they envy. There is no other means of escape. You can never release yourself by your own efforts – that's the first rule of the game.

You may try to use the very force of your Envy to lever yourself out of your unenviable position. You may, for example, if your Envy is all-consuming, become a revolutionary. In the opinion of the established, all revolutionaries are actuated by Envy. But the most successful revolutionary of this kind – and there have been many – may well see his hopes destroyed by the absurd idealists with whom he has to work - men who have some ridiculous vision of a changed order, whereas all he wishes is to take over the old one. Even if his sort of revolution wins the day, which it usually does, he is no better off, for he knows too well the signs of Envy not to be aware of the glint in the younger comrades' eyes; and he begins to envy his former security. And thus it is with the more conservative, individualist envier who uses the heat of his Envy to blaze a trail from log cabin to White House. It has not needed Mr Braine to suggest the torments at the Top.

Envy may be the motive force of social movement. It is also the reason why we have so little social originality; for Envy can never be creative, only imitative. So the envious boy must join the rat-race, and the envious girl, too. If she settles for marriage, her Envy may turn to the simple day-to-day pangs of keeping up with the Joneses.

These immediate, more material feminine envies are sometimes smiled at by the ambitious as petty, narrowranged; yet the truth is that Envy has a wonderful power to reduce the loftiest ambitions to a petty scale. It doesn't much matter whether your face turns green on reading a letter from Number 10, or at a certain page of *The Times*, or at the management's typed notice on the office wall – you still have the lurid look lit by the fires of hell. It doesn't much matter if you rise to your feet to congratulate Brown in the Mess Room, or the Senior Common Room, or at the local – your hearty laugh will still carry strange echoes of the cries of the damned.

Ambitious clergymen, service officers and shopstewards appear to suffer most, but this is surely a freak of the spotlight. After all, for some, such as actors and writers, Envy is so endemic that they have to adapt their lives to it. In these professions there is often no longer a concern to disguise the emotion, only to serve it up more palatably. Green Room cries are surely hardly intended to be taken seriously – 'Darling, you were wonderful. I hope the blissful play runs for ever and ever' is said with a sort of formalized wink to the company which invites complicity with the envious congratulator in his declared insincerity.

Simple envious women too – I mean here not those who have joined the careers rat-race, but covetous house-wives, dress-envious beauties, frustrated lion-hunting hostesses – often have the simple wisdom to adopt some such formalized cries to carry them through their nasty moments. I suspect that such caricatured insincerity, or, at least, a ridiculed version of the Envy one feels, is the best that the poor envious can do to avoid being an object of disgust. 'That lovely hat, darling! No, I mean it. Well look at my face. It's green'; such simple words invest the truth with a certain charm, and even make the envied woman appear somehow a little shameful for wearing a hat that arouses such painful emotions. It is certainly the only possible channel between the rocky coasts of grimacing pretence and graceless sulking.

Some, it is true, have tried the charm of open admission. I know an author who greets the success of others by saying quite truthfully 'I wished you dead when I read that good notice your book got last Sunday.' But however endearingly rueful the grin that accompanies it, there is something too consciously violent here in the treatment of convention; be open rudeness done never so easily, it nearly always suggests a struggle within the speaker that he would do better to conceal. Almost all the other deadly sins can be made to sound charming – pride has its rights, anger its justice, *acedia* its world-weary languor, lust its manly necessity and gluttony its boyish absurdity – but Envy never wins more than the sympathy that stokes the burning fires.

And yet I inevitably find myself trying to gain sympathy for the envious. In part this is, of course, a search for sympathy for the Envy in myself. Very few are without Envy, and no writer is without a good share of it. But the desire to condone extends beyond myself. Those wilful, beautiful orphan girls of Victorian novels who were consumed by their Envy for the spoilt darlings up at the hall – who can blame them? It was all very well for Mr Meagles to urge Tattycoram to count twenty-four, but why should she not be transported with rage at the sight of the adored Pet Meagles, no more beautiful than herself, and a great deal less interesting?

It is worth noting that the envious always feel themselves more 'interesting' than those they envy, who possess only the obvious graces like beauty, wit, money and good luck. This is but natural, for 'interesting' suggests a half-hidden wealth, virtues still only potential, and the envious must exist on belief in their potentialities, since Envy makes nothing for them of anything they achieve. But, to return to Tattycoram and other underprivileged girls, there is a simple reason for deploring their Envy; by it they are paralysed in sterile emotions, because of it they are unable to assert their claims to recognition.

And so it is, I suppose, with all the underprivileged, the old poor, the new poor, the crippled, the loveless, the socially outcast, the ugly, the boring and those who spit when they speak – and there can't be many of us who can opt out of all these categories; anyone who has no compassion for our grievances has lost humanity, but anyone who palliates our Envy seeks to destroy us. The most absurd yet frightening Envy in fiction, I believe, was created by Hugh Walpole in *The Old Ladies*. It is possible to sympathize with the fat, lonely old woman who wanted the silly old maid's amber so much that she frightened her to death. But if we go farther in our

sympathy and extend it to her Envy, we not only find
ourselves making light of the silly old maid's fright, so
terrible that it killed her, but we accept the awful dis-
torted face of the old woman in her envious lust. If we
followed such aesthetic guides in our reprobation of
Envy we should not go far wrong, for Envy, again,
wears an uglier face than lust's bloodshot eyes, or
gluttony's paunch, or pride's camel nose, or avarice's
thin lips.

This can be seen in the most distressing, foolish Envy
of our time – anti-Americanism in Western Europe. To
me European anti-Americanism is plain silly because
it is suicidal, but there are, after all, not only Communist
but tolerably argued neutralist views about this, and at
times American policy inclines one to sympathize with
such views. There are grievances against America which
deserve consideration from everyone. But anti-Americanism is quite another thing; it is an impotent Envy
which does nothing but disgrace the speaker. Listen to
any county Englishman or his wife who in dislike of
the changed English social order seeks refuge in anti-
American talk, hear the silly bray of their laugh, the
frightened note that underlies their jokes about American brashness or crudity. Or, almost worse, hear a group
of rich, beleaguered French or Italian or Spanish describing the necessity for a civilized Europe where
American barbarism cannot interfere. There are
few more nauseating sounds in the modern world;
nauseating because like all envious sounds they make
one feel ashamed for the emotions that the speaker is
betraying. And the same goes for anti-Russianism
where it is solely built on hopeless Envy.

That, of course, is why Envy is so unenviable a

dominating emotion. All the seven deadly sins are self-destroying, morbid appetites, but in their early stages at least lust and gluttony, avarice and sloth know some gratification, while anger and pride have power, even though that power eventually destroys itself. Envy is impotent, numbed with fear, yet never ceasing in its appetite; and it knows no gratification save endless self-torment. It has the ugliness of a trapped rat that has gnawed its own foot in its effort to escape.

PRIDE

PRIDE

Edith Sitwell

RIDE has always been one of my favourite virtues. I have never regarded it, except in certain cases, as a major sin.

Owing to a gradual debasement, a weakening of language, certain words do not, at this time, bear their original meaning. The word Pride is sometimes used when what is meant is a silly, useless vanity. Nor have I an affection for a pride which is simply the result of obstinacy.

There is, of course, a deadly sin of Pride – that which caused Hitler to say, 'I walk with the certainty of the somnambulist.' But there is also the Pride which can yet inspire love and admiration, such as Dante felt for his dear former tutor Brunetto Latini (said Professor Jacques Maritain in that great book, *Creative Intuition in Art and Poetry*), who even in Hell 'seemed like him who wins and not him who loses.'

Such was the tragic grandeur of

> *. . . that first archetype*
> *Of pride the paragon of all creation*
> *Who, of the light impatient, fell unripe.*
> DANTE: Paradiso XIX

A very great man (one of the greatest of our time) is reputed, I do not know with how much truth, to have said that his political opponents (who simply would not move and get out of the way, but persisted in being obstructions to every form of progress) were 'lion-hearted limpets'. I hope he said it. If he did not, he deserved to have said it, for the description could not be bettered. I have never been a limpet, lion-hearted or otherwise. My pride, which is great, is not of the kind that forbids me to move from any untenable position.

I have never minded being laughed at. All original artists *are* laughed at. But sometimes I laugh back, and that is not appreciated.

When I was a very young woman, I sat to Roger Fry (a most delightful man) for several portraits. Our appearance, as we crossed from his studio to his house for luncheon, caused a certain amount of interest. Roger wore, over his bushy grey hair, a very wide felt hat. I wore a leaf-green evening dress. With the result that the younger members of the crowd surveying us inquired:

A: 'Where did you get that hat,
     Where did you get that tile?'
B: 'Does your mother know you're out?'

– and, finally, suggested, benevolently, that a certain day in November would have been a more suitable day for our appearance.

Apropos of this date in November, my grandmother, Lady Londesborough, a most formidable lady, was the centre-piece of one of the worst falls from pride that I remember. It happened on that auspicious day, the Fifth of November. My grandmother was sitting in a bathchair, surrounded by captive daughters, outside the gate of the Londesborough Lodge gardens.

A young curate approached, accompanied by his wife. Struck by my grandmother's remarkable appearance, and remembering the date, he placed two pennies in her lap, and made his way into the gardens (which were private). The gift was *not* appreciated. In fact, there was an appalling storm, and the donor was chased by foot-men through the gardens.

I have always enjoyed those frequent occasions on which I have been put in a place that is not mine. When

I was about twenty-two years old, I went to a house belonging to some very rich people, in order to play the accompaniments on the piano for Helen Rootham, an admirable musician who had been engaged to sing at an afternoon party.

When the music was over, I was hastily removed from the drawing-room, as it was not thought suitable that I should have tea with gentry. The butler advanced upon me, 'Follow me, if you please, Miss.' And I found myself in a small room where, I must admit, a most delicious tea was awaiting me – everything that a girl of twenty-two would enjoy most – meringues, chocolate éclairs, etc. Of these I ate a great many. Then the butler reappeared, and I was led back into the drawing-room in order to accompany Helen on her farewell tour of the gentry.

There were a few moments of desultory conversation before the farewells were over.

'I do hope,' said my hostess's daughter, 'that Lady Londesborough is going to invite me to her ball.' (Lady Londesborough was the wife of my mother's brother, and was, at that time, one of the most important London hostesses.)

'I'll remind her,' I said. 'Lord Londesborough is my uncle, and I am staying with them at the moment.'

There was a short silence. Then we said goodbye.

I have never seen any of the gentry since.

It is sad when one's pride, which may be a form of love – perhaps one of the highest forms of love – receives a fall. When I was four years old, before the birth of either of my brothers, my pride and love were concentrated on the Renishaw peacock. This love was, *at the moment*, returned.

Every morning, punctually at nine o'clock (it is strange how birds and animals have an accurate sense of time), the peacock would stand on the leads outside my mother's bedroom, waiting for me to come and say good morning to her. When he saw me, he would let out a harsh shriek of welcome. (I do not, as a rule, appreciate ugly voices, but I loved him so much that in this case I did not care.) He would wait until I left my mother's room, and then, with another harsh shriek, would fly down into the garden to wait for me. We would walk round and round the large garden, not arm in arm, since that was impossible, but side by side, with my arm round his lovely shining neck. If it had not been for his crown, which made him slightly taller than me, we should have been of exactly the same size.

My nurse said to me, 'Why do you love Peaky so much?'

I replied 'Because he is beautiful and wears a heavenly crown.'

– 'The pride of the peacock,' wrote William Blake, 'is the glory of God.'

This lovely innocent romance lasted for months. Then my father found Peaky a wife, after which he never looked at me, but occupied himself completely with teaching his children to unfurl the fans with which they had been endowed for tails. I do not think it was the injury to my pride, being jilted by a peacock, that I minded. It was the injury to my affections.

True pride has no connection with the stupid vanity of the person who believes the world was created for his convenience, or to prove some theory of his.

'I am afraid, sir,' said the young author in *Lavengro*, 'it was very wrong to write such trash, and yet more, to allow it to be published.'

'Trash! Not at all,' replied his publisher. 'A very pretty piece of speculative philosophy. Of course you were wrong in saying there is no world. The world must exist, to have the shape of a pear. And that the world is shaped like a pear, and not like an apple, as the fools of Oxford say, I have satisfactorily proved in my book. Now, if there were no world, what would become of my system?' (Incidentally, if I remember rightly, in *The First Five Books of America*, we read that at one moment Christopher Columbus believed the world was shaped like a pear.)

In Mr Malcolm Letts's remarkable book about the real or imaginary Sir John Mandeville, he speaks of the belief held by medieval geographers that 'Jerusalem was the centre of the earth . . . Mandeville was concerned about the Antipodes because of the suggestion by the supporters of the flat earth theory that if, in fact, the earth were a sphere, the men on the sides and lower surface, would be living sideways or upside down, even if they did not fall off into space. . . . As Mandeville implies, if a man thinks he is walking upright, he is in fact walking the right way up, as God meant him to do, and that is all that matters.' This delightful suggestion seems to me to hold endless possibilities for the exercise of pride, and also conceit.

There is also a want of proper pride – which is ugly and evil, and ugly humility.

Blake said, 'Modesty is only the cloak of pride.'

I regard with disfavour the natural crawler – persons like the North American Indian who, according to Charleston's *Histoire de la Nouvelle France*, was found fondling a dead mouse, in the hope of appeasing the genius of mice.

When, after the Serpent's intolerable interference in the Garden of Eden, the Lord God said to him, 'Upon thy belly shalt thou go,' surely the Serpent was being condemned to an ugly form of humility.

I despise anything which reduces the pride of Man. In January, 1959, I read in a daily paper that in a certain town, 'A plan to lock a man in a cage for eight days and put him in a show in a public park as the carnival feature, is to be put before the Health Committee. . . . He would stay in the 12 feet by 12 feet cage day and night, the town's Carnival Committee was told.' The Carnival Committee's secretary said . . . 'We are looking for a volunteer who will play the part of a human ape. We will offer him a gratuity of £25, plus food, during the eight days and nights he will lie in the cage. Feeding times will be posted up outside the cage as in a zoo.'

I find it difficult to express my feelings about this hideous debasement of the pride of mankind.

We may remember, also, the praise bestowed upon an actress in America, of whom a critic wrote: 'Now I'm saying she will be the sensation of New York . . . she walked off the stage on all fours, with elbows and knees straighter than pokers.'

Is it *really* necessary to walk on all fours?

We should, like Goethe, regard man as 'the first conversation that nature holds with God.' And if this does not give us proper pride, we deserve to go with the gait of the Serpent.

Pride may be my own besetting sin; but it is also my besetting virtue. I take pride in the glory of mankind, and it would please me to think that like the Horse of which God spoke to Job, 'my neck is clothed with thunder.' (Wyclif dwarfed this, in his translation, down

to 'don about his necke with neiynge.') Certainly my
life has been spent in saying 'Ha ha among the trumpets.'

A *proper* pride is a necessity to an artist in any of the
arts. Only this will save an artist's work and his private
life from the attacks and intrusions made on these by
those unfortunate persons who have been unable to
attract attention to themselves except by incessant
bawling. Alexander Pope wrote in a letter:

'I will venture to say that no man ever rose to any
degree of perfection in writing, but through obstinacy and an inveterate resolution against the
stream of mankind; so that if the world has received
any benefit from the labours of the learned, it was in
its own despite. For when first they essay their parts,
all people in general are prejudiced against new
beginners: and when they have got a little above
contempt, then some particular persons who were
before unfortunate in their own attempts are sworn
foes to them only because they succeed.'

Socrates said to some carping person, 'I would rather
die having spoken in my manner, than speak in your
manner and live.'

This is the proper pride of the artist.

Iago is, I think, the greatest epitome in all literature
of wicked pride. This is his element, his climate, his
eternity, the whole of his being.

'If of that which this heart of mine is feeling, one
drop were to fall into hell, hell itself would become all
life eternal. . . .' Thus spoke St Catherine of Genoa . . .
the life eternal is union with God.

One drop from the pride of Iago would raise all hell
to rebellion against God. But that drop from the pride

of Iago would come from a heart that had no feeling.
He would, indeed, hardly know the difference between
those pains and the pleasures of heaven. For he is not a
damned soul. He is a devil.

Much of Shakespeare is concerned with the humbling
of pride, as in certain speeches of Hamlet:

> A man may fishe with the Worme that hath eat of
> a King, and eat of the fishe that had fed of that
> Worme.
>
> KING: What dost thou meane by this?
>
> HAMLET: Nothing but to show you how a King
> may goe a Progresse through the guts of a Begger.
>
> *Hamlet* iv, 3.

But death has its pride, as well as its humility.
Epiharnus of Syracuse (who was in his prime between
485 and 467 B.C.) told of a dead man saying 'I am a
corpse. A corpse is dung, and dung is earth. Earth is a
God; than am I not a corpse, but a God.'

The greatest poet of our time, W. B. Yeats, writing of
pride in humility, said:

> *O what a sweetness strayed*
> *Through barren Thebaid*
> *Or by the Mareotic sea*
> *When that exultant Anthony*
> *And twice a thousand more*
> *Starved upon the shore*
> *And withered to a bag of bones!*
> *What had the Caesars but their thrones?*

COVETOUSNESS

The Downfall of Jonathan Edax

COVETOUSNESS

Cyril Connolly

'Aᴀғᴛᴇʀ all, Jonathan, you can't take it with you.' At lunch, yesterday – Friday – from Brenda, that hoary old cliché again. It set me thinking. Of course, logistically, one couldn't. There's no point in actually being buried with the loot like Tutankhamen, though I would enjoy the sight of my coffin being followed to the vault by a procession of packing-cases and tea-chests. Crated rather than cremated. 'For the present, if nobody minds, I'm quite content to stay here.'

But, come to think of it, there *is* a way of taking it with one, and that is to endow the whole thing as a museum. One preserves one's name, and it keeps the collection together. More than one dare expect from one's own family. They shall have front seats at the opening – if they can get away from their jobs. I can picture their faces. I'm certainly not going to take *them* with me:

The Edax Foundation: A small closed collection, museum and library open thrice yearly to the general public, with microfilm material available to accredited students. Endowed by Mr Jonathan Edax, this small closed collection contains some of the choicest examples of etc, etc, illustrating the taste and discrimination of its munificent founder. A fitting memorial to the days when it was still possible for one man, etc, etc. . . .

'The human eye deteriorates all it looks at' – whoever wrote that should be my first Curator. Museum. Mausoleum. Except on the three annual viewing days the collection should be kept in permanent darkness. Pharaoh would have approved. But what about tomb-robbers? Photoscopic devices, the most up to date in existence, give instant warning of the minutest disturbance, such as the flashing of a light.

But these are morbid thoughts. My collections are incomplete. And I am still here to complete them. I shall go round to little Truslove. He's sure to be away.

Thomas Truslove. My oldest friend. Once a most gifted young poet, he is now completely forgotten and spends all his time on television, editorial boards, P.E.N. Club activities, book of the month clubs and American lecture tours. Last week in Buffalo, this week in Rome – he only comes to England in his sabbatical year. But – and this is the point – he continues to be deluged with every pamphlet, every privately printed book that comes out. You can find anything at Truslove's. When I go round I always take a second edition of something or a second issue, or a defective copy, and substitute it, when his back's turned, for the right one. To him that hath shall be given. He never notices, only likes painting, anyway. Sometimes he tries most generously to present me with my own rejections, the ignorant booby. Today I took round a second edition of Hopkins. Virginia Truslove opened the door.

'You've come to see Thomas? He's in Borneo. But he'll be back tomorrow morning. We're lunching with the Clarks.' I gave her the gimlet gaze. 'I've come to see *you*.' Virginia was what some people would consider 'still a beautiful woman.' She looked rather flustered. '*Mille grazie*! Do come in.' I put down my coat in the hall and walked straight into the library. 'Would you like some tea?'

'Nothing better. I'd give my soul for a nice cup of tea – the way you always make it.' 'I'll get it myself.'

It always works! Drinks, no – too often they're on the table. But tea!

'I'd give my soul for it' – and down she goes to the basement. Ten clear minutes and always a warning rattle on the way back!

Sure enough, there was the right Hopkins – 1918. The exchange was the work of a moment, and I dived into the pamphlets: 'Poems written in discouragement', only fifty copies – 'to my young friend Thomas the Rhymer, W. B. Yeats.' 'Prufrock and other observations,' – 'To Thomas from Tom.'

I didn't know where to begin. Even in my inside jacket pocket a slim volume might run a slim risk of being detected. 'Dear Thomas, Even you won't dare to print this, Ezra.' Jiminy cricket! Which shall it be – or why not all three?

Oh!

'Wasn't I quick! That's the electric kettle. I hope you haven't been too bored.'

'Just leafing through a few of Thomas's old circulars.'

'Aren't they a nuisance? As soon as he comes back we're going to have a thorough clean-out. Books are bad enough – but manuscripts, letters – he's kept *everything*.'

'Would you like me to go through them for you?'

'How angelic – but why should you do all this for me?'

'For an excellent reason.' And I looked down at her with my gimlet glance.

'There ought to be a law against it. Look at this one – "With some trepidation, Dylan". Why can't all these poets let poor Thomas alone. Nobody can print anything without inflicting a copy on him. He's like the British Museum.'

'I could start right now.'

'We'd better wait till he comes back. We might throw away a drawing by mistake. He won't be long. He's only gone to deliver a message at a conference.'

'In Borneo?'

'He's beamed at the Orient, you know.'

'Fortunate fellow!'

She put the pamphlets back in the glass-fronted bookcase and set the tea-tray on the table. Damned interference.

When I got home with my Hopkins, Brenda was waiting.

'Jonathan – where have you *been?*'

'Went to return a book to old Truslove.'

'Caroline's fallen downstairs.'

'Did she hurt herself?'

'No, thank God. Not this time.'

'Well then, it's not very important.'

'It happens to be important, because she fell downstairs because you won't put up a gate, and you won't put up a gate because you're too mean to spend three pounds on one because all your money goes on candlesticks and teapots and filthy old books and china and glass and furniture and silver and candlesticks and teapots.'

Teapots! It's quite true I had been too busy with that bookcase to have a proper look. The Trusloves were just the kind of people to inherit some Queen Anne. Back to the Trusloves first thing tomorrow!

'Teapots with no tea, decanters with no wine, centrepieces for non-existent dinners – and Caroline could break her neck for all you'd care.'

'Why don't you get the gate yourself?'

'Out of what *you* give me?'

Now I happened to have read that small children have a very good sense of self-preservation even when descending stairs, and that if they do fall their little bodies, with so much fat and water content, are extraordinarily resilient. I shut myself into my study and accommodated Hopkins – 'I am gall, I am heartburn' – among my 'Recent Acquisitions'.

A few minutes later the telephone rang: 'It's me, Virginia. I'm so worried. Thomas has just cabled he's stopping off at Jakarta to judge some Indonesian Abstracts. He'll be late for the Clarks and miss his Lit. Soc. What shall I do?'

'You'd better take me with you.' 'Oh, what a good idea! Jon, you're so thoughtful for me!'

I remembered that I hadn't quite finished my egg at luncheon and retired to the pantry. The Clarks! *Veritable cave d'Aladdin.* My luck was in. I found the egg and went back to my study. When I stand up before my largest bookcase I call it 'being at the Controls'. I feel like a captain on the bridge, or Sandy Macpherson at his Wurlitzer. I expect the whole thing to sink down through the floor at the end of my virtuoso performance.

This evening I took out the keys of the plate-chests, then I inspected the green and yellow Sèvres, the Vincennes, the Chelsea and some of the Meissen, and went back to the Controls again. That Yeats, that Eliot, that Auden manuscript, perhaps weighed a few ounces between them, occupied the same space as one bad novel, yet were worth several hundred pounds and represented for me the conclusion of years of search and patient effort. Good old Truslove – if he'd only been born a few years earlier and had been given *Mosada* or *A Lume Spento*.

God's most deep decree
Bitter would have me taste. My taste was me.
I couldn't get Hopkins out of my head. 'My taste was me' – what a title for an autobiography! And when one's taste is flawless – near-perfect, and matched by a nose and an eye for a bargain and a bump of curiosity and righteous ambition to spoil the Philistine, there's no end to what one can pick up. To know what someone else values is to be already on the way to possessing it.

Saturday: Today I woke with a tiny worry. On the landing I heard Brenda and Caroline: 'One two three four, one and two and three and four,' no doubt a charming maternal tableau. Then I remembered. Why hadn't I noticed the teapot? After our lunch we must go back there. And I would take a few old copies of *Horizon* and *Penguin New Writing* to stuff up any gaps I made in the tidying.

With silver and china it's not so easy. One can't 'borrow' somebody's dinner service or pocket a *garniture de cheminée*. One has to learn to carry cash and make unpredictable offers. Carry cash! That hurts. Still, I am a gentleman, and a gentleman is someone who can reasonably expect to live in the same style and demand the same treatment as his forefathers in a society which has gone completely haywire. The world owes me a living, says the parasite. No. I owe myself a living, says the gentleman. Let Edax hold what Edax held; and a little bit over for safety.

Telephone! 'It's me, Virginia. Jonathan, I'm so worried I've rung up the Clarks and they'd rather the lunch was put off till Thomas got back. And now I've no one to lunch with today.' The skinflints. To hell with all of them.

'Well, lunch you know is never very easy for me. But perhaps we can meet afterwards.'

'But if you were free to lunch with the Clarks I thought perhaps you might . . .'

'And get poisoned in one of those filthy restaurants? I see a man got thrombosis from Scallops Mornay.'

'Well then – you must come and lunch here. I'll have to see what I can do with my own fair fingers. But don't expect the Crown Derby.'

'You have some Crown Derby?'

'Well, I don't know what it is, of course . . .'

Why do they all say *of course*?

'. . . But I do know it's fearfully old and Granny thought the world of it. It's supposed to be terribly valuable.'

'It sounds like Mason's Ironstone.'

'What's that?'

'I said we'll have to turn it over and look at the marks.'

'No need to be improper.'

'Very well then, one o'clock.'

Silly bitch. The last woman I took out to lunch cost me £12,000 for four words. Well, with her 'Yes' you could say it made five words. I could still hear her in the next room, with her kitchen cough, moving about and making lists of all the things that she and Caroline 'simply had to have' – shoes, shirts, sheets, socks, chocs, each item more perishable than the last – and the Spanish girl with her list, too. Thank God there was one sane person in this household of crazy women.

The Edax Endowment. A Thought at the Controls; some of my books – some of the rarest – have other people's book-plates, coats of arms, country-house

libraries; people with country-house libraries are among
the biggest suckers in existence. Should I leave the
book-plates in? Or steam them off? Or leave it to the
executors? But who are my executors? Do I know a
single person who isn't a bloody fool? One might choose
an heir by examination. My will would be an examination paper. Or a treasure-hunt. But with all these
bibliographies flying around they'd be bound to cheat.
But to-day I shall put it aside, I feel sound as a Getty –
and all a-tingle for the chase.

'Jonathan – where are you *going?*'

'Out to lunch – for a change.'

'But your egg.'

'Stuff it.'

'And the shopping-money.'

'Borrow from the Spanish girl.'

'Jonathan. Do you realize you haven't paid her wages
for three weeks. Caroline's shoes are worn out. Do you
expect us to live on air – when do you think I last went
to the hairdresser?'

'Oh for God's sake. Get a long-playing record of
yourself and send it to the Naggers' Club. Best years of
your life. Worn your fingers to the bone. Waiting on
me hand and foot. All the jazz.'

The usual screams and yowls, in which Caroline joins
with automatic mimicry. Thank God somebody keeps
his head in this bedlam. Luckily I had chosen my cane
and so had no further cause to linger. I blessed the
Fermier-Général who had selected the perfectly
fitting gold pommel with the reassuring *chinoiserie*, and
I blessed the country-house croquet set where I had
found it.

The Spanish girl! Once the Trusloves' proudest

possession – nothing she wouldn't do – laundry, mending, no evenings out. I soon got my eye on her. Took a bit of winkling, too – I told her that her employers were atheists who would probably poison her. Brenda is a Catholic, you see. Marriage is a life-sentence with her. So I give – and expect – no quarter. I had to go to church myself, just to convince the *chica*, and listen to the sermon. 'Nor his ox nor his ass nor his manservant nor his maidservant.' All the jazz. These Spaniards! Eat you out of house and home!

One of my grievances against old Truslove is that he would choose to live halfway between two fare-stages. One either has a goodish walk, or has to go on and break into a coin. Luckily it was a fine day.

Virginia opened the door. 'Look at him. Isn't he smart! With the hat and the cane and the Sherlock Holmes profile. Positively satanic.'

Damned impertinence. 'You don't look too bad yourself.' She was what our ancestors called a handsome woman, chivalrously adding 'very fine eyes.' Poor Truslove. Twenty years of marriage, say a pound a week to feed her and another for pin-money – thousands of pounds down the drain. Every woman after forty is a wasting asset.

'I know how you love beautiful things. I've got out all my treasures.' We sat down to a fricassee of chicken and a bottle of rosé. King's Pattern everywhere; all the silver was heavily embossed and the Crown Derby was quite respectable Coalport. 'The place for good china is under lock and key.' I wagged an admonitory finger, 'And now, since you've spoilt me so thoroughly, may I make one more request?'

'Granted as soon as asked.'

'Can we have tea instead of coffee?' She looked rather sadly at the Cona machine. 'I'll go and make it myself.' Five minutes to go, with that damned electric kettle. I made a rush at the bookcase. It was locked. It was one of those big mahogany efforts, and there, behind the glass, I could see all the presentation copies and the enigmatic plain backs of the slimmer volumes. It wasn't really locked, I discovered, only jammed, otherwise I should have felt deeply insulted. I gave a good pull and the whole front came away; the hinges had gone. A sheet of glass fell forward and splintered round my head, badly cutting the hand which I raised to protect it. Virginia entered with the tray – 'Oh you poor thing – let me bandage it. You must have a tourniquet. Why, you've bled all over the manuscripts.'

It was true. 'Thomas – even you won't dare to print this' had become completely illegible. She thrust a pamphlet in my pocket – 'Here, have one of these for luck.' And then I spotted the teapot. It was hexagonal, genuine Queen Anne. I even got it up high enough to see the Britannia standard. One would commit murder for such a piece – or worse. What havoc it would wreak among my Georgian urns and melons! It would run to thousands.

'Jonathan,' said Virginia, 'I've been wanting to talk to you for a very long time. You're not happy, are you?' I gave her the old gimlet. 'Poor old Jon – you can't deceive me. You see I know all about you and Brenda.' 'There's nothing to know.' 'Yes – that's just what I do know – and I know you only married her because she was engaged to Thomas.' 'Virginia——' 'And when you took Brenda – can't you see, Jonathan – there was nothing left for me to do but marry him.' 'Virginia——'

'Stop – and I know too what a marriage with nothing is like because that's what mine is. Married to a poster, a voice on a dictaphone, an airplane reservation. We can't go on like this, Jonathan. I'm forty now and you must be . . .' 'Virginia!' 'Wait – don't worry – you shall have me. You've been so sweet, so patient, so under-standing – coming always to see me when he's out – yet never a word disloyal to him, always his best friend. Don't think I haven't noticed, dispelling my loneliness, my emptiness – and you so big, so quiet, so kind.' 'Virginia!' 'Wait – silly. I'm all yours now. Listen. I've cabled: "Don't hurry back. Clark's lunch postponed. All Well – Virginia." Now aren't I rather clever!'

'Virginia – the teapot. Whose is it?' 'Mine, you silly-billy. Do you think we would be drinking tea out of it at this moment if it were his. Do you think I wouldn't protect your chivalry. Whither I go, it goes – my dowry – it will be about all I have. There used to be a silly old kettle on a stand as high as myself.' 'Virginia, I feel faint. My wrist. I must see a doctor. No, I can walk, thank you.'

Once in the street I pulled out the pamphlet she had given me. Unbelievable – the ultimate rarity! *The Bourbon Rose and other poems*, by Alberic Chute. Privately printed, Newport Pagnell, 1886. His first book – of which up till now only two copies were known, Hayward's and the Bodleian's. Alberic Chute, that exquisite talent, silenced it was said by some evil tentacle of the Wilde scandal after his third and most remarkable book of poems. He would be nearly ninety now, if this post-Raphaelite pre-Imagist were alive . . .

If he were alive! Why not – and if he is alive then he shall inscribe *The Bourbon Rose* for me and I will

possess a better copy than either of the others. I made
for a telephone box. There he was! Alberic Chute,
Squire's Mount, Hampstead. Should I ring up to make
sure? Often the worst of all methods. First they hang
up on you, and then they won't let you in. Desperate
occasions require desperate remedies. I took a taxi.
When I rang the bell there was a commotion. The door
was opened by an elderly man. 'Can I see Mr Chute?'
'Mr Chute is very ill indeed and can see no one.' 'The
matter is extremely urgent.' 'I am afraid any question
of urgency is now purely relative.' The last word gave
me a clue. 'You see, I am his son.' 'Mr Chute was unmarried.' 'That is my tragedy, not his.' 'Your name.'
'It would mean nothing. Here are my credentials.' I
held up the book to him. 'Newport Pagnell – yes – he
did live there, for a very considerable time. Well, you
had better come in. I am Doctor Prout.'

He led me through to a room on the ground floor.
'I should warn you it may come at any moment. My
patient is in uraemia.'

It was a small sitting-room with no good pieces into
which a brass bed had recently been moved. On this
was lying a tiny old man with closed eyes and a nose
like a tin-opener, his hands milking the coverlet. A
nurse was standing by. She held a finger to her lips.
With my cane in my bandaged hand and *The Bourbon
Rose* in the other I tiptoed over.

I have managed to live more years than I care to
consider without any close experience of death. There
is nothing in such a phenomenon to appeal to the
collector. The foot-hills of Death and Love are, however, hunting-grounds for such of us as lay up treasure
on earth and pursue enduring artefacts rather than the

illusions of common humanity. I have often found a long face at a memorial service lead to substantial pickings.

I was brooding on certain gaps that still needed closing before my serried ranks of Americana could be brought up to battle strength when the nurse disappeared behind a screen. Almost immediately the sick man opened his eyes and seemed to want to sit up. He favoured me with a penetrating stare. I brandished *The Bourbon Rose* before him and reached for my pen; but to do that I had to lean the cane against the bed and a rash movement of his caused it to slip so that the heavy gold knob with its mandarins and pagodas fell with a clatter on the parquet. With glaring eye the old poet tried to heave himself up and thrust forward, his hand jerking at me as the nurse rushed round. 'You—' he gasped and fell backward. I had enough presence of mind as the doctor entered to retrieve my cane and sink my head on my arms. 'My father . . .'

I was more than relieved to get away on a pretext that I had to telephone, and I had run quite a distance from Squire's Mount, my black felt hat in one hand, my cane in the other, before I realized that I had left *The Bourbon Rose* behind. Agony! I felt such a stinging sense of loss that I could almost have wept. The greedy old bastard!

By felicitous combinations of the London Transport system I made my way home, for I pined to be at the Controls again. My reference library alone is more extensive than all the books to be found in an ordinary household; it starts in my bedroom and spills over the upper landing. I can trace the mark on a piece of china, the owners of a crest, the rubric of a goldsmith, the succeeding possessors of a book or manuscript, the vicissitudes of some piece in the saleroom, in a matter of minutes. They are the jig-tools of my occupation.

Before letting myself in I sent off three cables to Truslove: care of P.E.N. Club, Jakarta; British Council, Singapore; and Nehru, Delhi. 'Clarks upfed threaten off-brush. Hurry!' Then I made a dash for the landing. Great God! At the top of the stairs a hideous little gate of white metal, stuck onto the wall at each side by suction-pads. For a household of hurdlers!

'Brenda', I shouted. She came out, smiling. 'I thought you'd be surprised. Now our daughter – for you seem to forget that she is yours as well as mine – can grow up without risking her life every few minutes.' 'How did you pay for it?' 'I charged it.' 'You have no account.' 'I put it down on yours.' 'You PUT IT DOWN!' I felt a lump of rage surge up and choke me, like when Caroline tore the book jackets. 'You filthy extravagant slut, I'll sue you.' 'Anal-erotic madman.' 'I'll put a notice in the papers. I'll hound you out of my house.'

The telephone rang in my bedroom. (I permit no outgoing calls.) 'It's me, Virginia. Darling. He's on his way back. We must leave at once. I'm desperate.' 'Impossible. I can't ever see you again.' 'Then I shall kill myself. Now.' 'Goodbye.' These crazy women! Suddenly I had a vision in all its leaden moonglow perfection of the little hexagonal teapot. Now was my chance. I ran out of my room and took a flying kick at that bloody gate.

'Aaaaaaaahh. . . .'

A verdict of death by misadventure was returned on Mr Jonathan Edax, the well-known connoisseur and collector who broke his neck by falling down the stairs at his home in Holland Park on Saturday night. The stairs were exceptionally steep and a gate had recently been installed at the top of them by Mrs Edax; it had presumably been insecurely attached. The deceased had appeared to be in a disturbed frame of mind at the prospect of making his will. Mr and Mrs Thomas Truslove were present at the inquest but were not called upon to give evidence. Jonathan Hagan Edax was born in 1895 at Bedford, where his father was a prosperous solicitor. After completing his studies, he had early made his mark in the correspondence columns of learned periodicals and was soon recognized as a formidable opponent in the auction room at a time when it was still possible for one man, etc, etc.

GLUTTONY

GLUTTONY

Patrick Leigh-Fermor

'GLUTTONY. Yes. Let me see.' Mr Vortigern paused in the pillared doorway to light a cigar, and his ruminative murmur was punctuated by puffs.

'*Voracitas* . . . Γαστριμαργια . . . *Gola* . . . *Gourmandise* . . . Yes. . . .' His cigar properly alight, he sailed down the steps to the sunlit street in an aromatic cloud. No one would have thought this hale and elegant figure was seventy-five.

'I have been a martyr to it, in a mild way, all my life,' he resumed as we headed for St James's Palace. 'So its presence among the Seven Deadly Sins has always bothered me. I console myself with the thought that Ambrose and Augustine – or was it St Clement – had monks in mind more than laymen when the Deadly Sins first emerged; and, of course, they needed some corrective to late Roman excesses and barbarian disorder.

'You only have to read about the *vomitoria* and Trimalchio's feast in Petronius to get the point. And what was the name of that senator who had slaves walking backwards in front of him to carry his paunch? And what about Pollio – Vedius, not Asinius – who lived in Naples in the time of Augustus? He used to punish his slaves by throwing them into the tank where he kept his fish because he thought that a diet of live humans improved the flavour. And barbarian banquets were filthy. Think of those raw slabs of meat the Huns used to strap between their saddle flaps and the flanks of their horses! Things had got out of hand.

'There's nothing against good living in itself. We have only to remember the Marriage at Cana. St Benedict allowed his monks a *hemina* of wine with their meals. And look at the distilling traditions of the monastic orders, and the description of the Abbot's meal in Phtochoprodromos, the Byzantine poet. There has always been a port-drinking Horace-quoting tradition in Anglican cathedral closes, and all those paintings of cardinals clinking glasses must be founded on something.'

Mr Vortigern's humorous agate eyes caught mine for a moment. 'Do you know the story the Romans are so fond of about a Pope – a fairly recent one too and a saintly man – at the gates of Paradise? You don't? Well, there is a tradition that St Peter stands aside, when a supreme Pontiff arrives, to allow his successor to let himself in with his own keys. This one, who was famous for his appreciation of wine, was embarrassed to find himself, after a lot of twisting and turning, still locked out.' Mr Vortigern laughed. 'He had brought the keys of the Vatican cellar by mistake. . . .

'What are the five ways of sinning by gluttony. . . .? *Praepropere*, *laute*, *nimis*, *ardenter*, *studiose?*' Mr Vortigern ticked them off on his fingers. 'Too soon, too expensively, too much, too eagerly, and making too much of a fuss. I am guilty on all points, alas; but at least I can be acquitted of St John of the Cross's Spiritual Gluttony. . . . Too much and too eagerly are the worst. I shudder to think of myself as a boy, reeling from the table stunned with toad-in-the-hole and sausages and mash and jelly and spotted dog, and steeped in sin. And the torments that followed! Hell on earth!

'Mercifully, a glimmer of moderation came with riper years. For, now that Science has disarmed Lust of its retaliatory powers, Gluttony is the only one of the

Deadly Seven which is visited by physical retribution this side of the tomb.

'Its vengeance is far more convincing than Dante's penalty for gluttons – permanent hounding by Cerberus in a non-stop hailstorm. Spiritual sins may rack the conscience, fill us with misery, lay the soul waste, and turn our hearts to stone. Alas, they do! But at least they don't ruin our blood pressure or hobnail our livers. What are snarling and hailstones compared with the pangs of indigestion, palpitations, muck-sweats, heartburn, bilious attacks, d.t.s, real alcoholism, nicotine poisoning? The Fathers didn't reckon with this.' Mr Vortigern flourished his cigar. 'What torments can match the agony of a chainsmoker short of tobacco? Surely these earthly pains and humiliations should shorten our sentences later on? And what about obesity, bottle-noses, bleary eyes, grog-blossoms and breath like a blowlamp? It is the only sin which turns us into monsters. I have got off lightly so far.' Mr Vortigern glanced with satisfaction at his reflection in a gunsmith's window. 'At least *girth*-control invites no anathema, if we can but practice it. Always remember that outside every thin man lurks a fat man trying to climb in.

'The Germans are the worst, for sheer bulk. What miles of liver sausage, what oceans of beer and quagmires of those colossal bellies! How appalling they look from behind; the terrible creases of fat three deep across solid and shaven napes! Necks wreathed in smiles, the stigmata of damnation; and delusive smiles, for when they turn round there is nothing but a blank stare and a jigsaw of fencing scars. If you are ever losing an argument with such a one you can always win by telling him to wipe those smiles off the back of his neck. . . .

'The outward effects of food are a sure guide. In England they are very noticeable. Prosperous Edwardians had an unmistakable ptarmigan sheen. There was beef and claret in the faces of the squirearchy, cabbage and strong Indian tea among Non-conformists, and limpid blue eyes in the Navy, due to Plymouth gin, and so on. Above all, a general look of low spirits that tells its own tale. Those puddings named after Crimean battles, that coffee that tastes like boiled horse-shoes. . . .!'

Mr Vortigern shuddered. 'Meals as joyless as a mouth's dark banquet in a cupboard. Everything tastes like a substitute. I think the flight from reality must have begun when Norman names superseded the Saxon after the Conquest – mutton for sheep, beef for ox, and so on – breaking into a gallop later on by the use of French in eating-houses. It culminates in those Bohemian little 'Continental' restaurants whose walls are festooned with papier mâché chickens, dummy mortadellas and cardboard hams, all too emblematic of the phantom food below. The English seek escape from this ghost world in sporting preoccupations and foreign enterprise and occasionally in poetry. It's the same with the Irish. Have you ever eaten an Irish meal? Their literature has nothing to do with oppression, religion or the twilight. It is flight from the cruel realities of the table.

'These are effects by reaction; direct results are still more striking. Curry induces instability of temper and fosters discord; hot Mexican food leads to cruelty, just as surely as blubber, the staple of the Eskimos, spells torpid indifference. And look at the Belgians, the supreme exemplars of high living and low thinking! The rancid oil they cook with in Spain tastes as though it was straight out of a sanctuary lamp; no wonder the country is prone to bigotry. Vodka turns Russian faces into steppes, featureless tundras with eyes like minute and uncharted Siberian lakes. And those extraordinary grey complexions of the Americans I attribute entirely to breakfast foods, jumbo steaks, soft drinks, milk shakes and ice-cream at all hours, washed down by conditioned air and crooning.'

Mr Vortigern's words had brought us to the Mall. We crossed into the park and he smoked thoughtfully for a minute. 'The most convincing example of the influence of food on national character is Italy. Look at Italian art. Pasta wrecked it! Some say it was imported from the Orient by Marco Polo. Others that an old woman discovered it in Naples in the time of Frederick II of Hohenstaufen, the *stupor mundi*. I favour the second theory. Cimabue and Giotto and Duccio lived on dried fish and polenta and beans and black bread and olives. And you can't picture Dante eating spaghetti, or Amico di Sandro wolfing ravioli down. They lived on hard tack from the Trecento to the Renaissance, you mark my words.

'Then *pasta asciutta* came. It must have taken a century or two to conquer Italy, spreading from the south like a clammy and many-tentacled monster, smothering Italy's genius on its northward journey, and strangling its artists like the serpents of Laocoön. Thousands of seething and dripping tongues of maca-roni squirming and coiling up the Apennines, gathering volume every mile, engulfing towns and provinces and slowly subduing the whole peninsula. The North held out heroically for a while – there is no pasta in those banquets of Veronese – and the last stand was at Venice. The rest of the country lay inert under its warm and slippery bonds – slippery, perhaps, but still unbroken today – while Tiepolo held out, and Longhi and Guardi and Canaletto, the last lonely frontiersmen of a fallen Empire.

'But one day some treacherous dauber must have swallowed a streaming green yard or two of *tagliatelle* – the end of the enemy's foremost tentacle, you might say – and, hotfoot, the rest of the huge, victorious monster came coiling into the Veneto and reared itself for the kill. And then——' the end of Mr Vortigern's malacca cane, which had been describing faster and faster loops in the air, stopped in mid-sweep – 'and then, wallop! A billion boiling tons of pasta fell on the town, and the proud city, the sea's bride, with her towers and domes and bridges and monuments and canals, went under. The piazzas were a tragic squirming tangle of spaghetti and lasagne, the lagoon ran red with tomato sauce. Italy's genius was dead, laid low by her own gluttony . . . not only Italy's painting, but Italian thought and poetry and literature and rhetoric and even Italian architecture. Everything was turned into macaroni.'

Mr Vortigern fell silent. The world seemed locked for a while in an elegiac hush. 'But,' he resumed at last, 'it had its compensations. Baroque's debt to pasta has never been fully recognized. In fountain statuary its influence was supreme. Think of those beautiful fountains at the Villa d'Este and Bagnaia! Think of the Piazza Navona and the Piazza di Trevi! Where do you think they found the inspiration for all those bearded

Tritons, those Neptunes and gushing river gods and sea
beasts, those swirling beards and fish tails and manes, all
ending in water weed? That feeling for tempestuous and
tangled flow, of deliquescence, of solidity in flux, that
brio and speed and sweep?

'Where but in those swirling ingurgitated forkloads,
those wild mealtime furlongs that keep a Roman going?
They are pure Bernini, an Italian dinner played backwards, Gorgon-struck in mid-swoop. . . . Conversely,
how eatable post-Renaissance Italian architecture looks
– scagliola rock cakes, Carrara barley sugar, marzipan
statuary, pasta in travertine, ceilings and cloudbursts
straight out of an icing-gun! It is not for nothing that
the Victor Emmanuel monument is called the Wedding
Cake. Perhaps,' Mr Vortigern continued with a change
of key, 'one should adopt a gastronomic approach to all
architecture, like a cannibal's attitude towards his
fellow mortals. The Taj Mahal would be delicious,
especially on a hot day. Gothic horrible; too bony. And
I would not care for a square meal of Corbusier, either.
Too square by half and far too austere. The food might
be concrete, I feel, and the drink abstract . . .

'Cannibalism is a problem. In many cases the practice
is rooted in ritual and superstition rather than gastro-
nomy, but not always. A French Dominican in the
seventeenth century observed that the Caribs had most
decided notions on the relative merits of their enemies.
As one would expect, the French were delicious, by
far the best. This is no surprise, even allowing for
nationalism. The English came next, I'm glad to say.
The Dutch were dull and stodgy and the Spaniards so
stringy, they were hardly a meal at all, even boiled. All
this sounds sadly like gluttony.

'France, you will agree, is the place where the instinct has been most successfully harnessed and exploited. But this pre-eminence exacts a cruel price. The liver! That is their Achilles heel! It is a national scourge, brought on by those delicious sauces, by all those truffles and chopped mushrooms peeping through the liquid beige. Every Frenchman over fifty writhes under its torments. He is a chained Prometheus, a victim of the tribal inventiveness. Only it's no vulture that pecks at the weak spot but the phantom and vengeful beaks of an army of geese from Strasbourg. Now the Chinese——'.

Mr Vortigern broke off. A mild flurry of excitement and a scatter of clapping reached our ears across the flower beds. We caught a glimpse of a long motor-car with a flag on the bonnet, and a gloved hand in the window fluttering in gracious acknowledgement. Mr Vortigern gravely raised his hat.

'Diet and royalty,' he said as he replaced it, 'there's a rewarding theme! Not only in our fortunate kingdom but all over Europe. It is the supreme illustration of the importance of regular meals over long periods. There's no question here of that unsettling swing between unwilling frugality and neurotic stuffing which has been the lot of most commoners. It is a matter of excellent meals in unfaltering continuity.

'Think of a chart of royal quarterings, each coat representing an ancestor and the number doubling with each receding generation; two parents, four grandparents, eight great-grandparents – sixteen, thirty-two, sixty-four, a hundred and twenty-eight, doubling each time – you've got over a thousand in only ten generations, and by the fourteenth century, counting four generations a century, over eight million.

'Eight million splendidly fed forbears! Turn this upside-down' – the ferrule of his cane drew an isosceles, the ferrule swept from left to right in an airy hypotenuse – 'and it becomes the base of a steaming pyramid of regular and wonderful meals – quadrillions of them! – on the apex of which each royal person is seated. Of course there are one or two hungry strains – the Bonapartes, perhaps, the Karageorgevitches and the Montenegrins – mountain life, you know, and the hardships of a pastoral calling – but the rest seldom skipped a meal. A religious ascetic here and there, I dare say, and perhaps a vegetarian or two in the last hundred years, but otherwise, it is an imposing edifice of breakfasts and luncheons and teas and dinners and, no doubt, delicious late suppers. A fragrant and unfailing counterweight to the cares of State.

'*It was all good stuff*, that is the point! And what is the result of this magnificent continuity? A much rarer quality than mere looks or brains or brawn, a priceless adjunct to outward splendour and inward dedication: no less than majesty itself. An indefinable aura, at the same time gracious, affable, untroubled, august, Olympian and debonair, to which few commoners and no chance-fed dictators or hungry and fortuitously nourished heads of state, whether beefy or scrawny, can possibly aspire. I hope you won't think me a reactionary or a snob when I say that these random figureheads have neither the breeding nor the feeding.

'I see by your puzzled brow,' Mr Vortigern continued, 'that you have spotted the fallacy in my theory. How could each of us have eight million ancestors in the fourteenth century – for we all have the same number, however obscure and hungry – when the population of

England after the Black Death was under a million? You conclude that most of them were the same. Rightly. They were pluralist progenitors. It narrows the triangle and inter-relates us all. Remember, too, that if we take up a fundamentalist position, this expanding fan must begin to taper at some point, finally dwindling to Adam and Eve: two pyramids stuck base to base forming a lozenge.

'Each of us is at the bottom of one of these huge human rhomboids.' He described one in the air with four malacca strokes. 'This means that sooner or later you are related to everyone in the island. A glorious and intimidating thought.' His stick, leaving the rhomboid in mid-air like an invisible hatchment, soared in ample sweeps, symbolizing universal kinship – and then fell static, aimed at a figure lying supine on the grass. A Herculean and bearded tramp, his boots removed and a stove-in bowler over his eyes, snored contentedly among the mandarin ducks and the sheldrakes. 'That grimy old boy is sure to be a relation of yours. And of mine too, of course. He looks as though he enjoys his food. I would dearly like to slip him a fiver. After all, blood is thicker than water. . . .'

We paused on the Regent's bridge, the crook of his stick safe over his arm once more while he lit a new cigar.

'But I fear I digress,' he resumed. His words were scanned by thoughtful puffs. 'It is odd that *solid* gluttony has inspired so small a literature – outside cookery books I mean – compared to its liquid form. There is Rabelais, of course, and the 'Eloge de la Gourmandise', and that amazing Norman guzzling in Flaubert, and there must be more. Des Esseintes' black banquet in Huysmans doesn't really count: it was aesthetic, and gastronomic. But there is no end to poems in praise of wine. Hundreds of them! And some of the best prose of our younger writers – Waugh and Connolly, for instance – is dedicated to it. Those beautiful similes! Wines that steal up to one like shy fawns, and other delightful comparisons! They are charming! Charming, but hopeless. These gifted writers face the same problem as mystics attempting to convey their experiences in the language of profane love.'

He watched a pelican preening its breast-feathers for a moment. 'What a pity the same device is so seldom used in a derogatory sense: Algerian that charges like a rhinoceros, port-types that draw alongside like charabancs, liqueurs that reek like a bombed scent factory! Yes, blame, as well as praise, should be codified. Michelin allots stars for merit, and rightly. We follow them across France like voracious Magi. Vortigern's Guide would have them, too, but also a scale of conventional signs to warn my readers. A bicarbonate pill first, then a basin, a stretcher, an ambulance and, finally, a tombstone.

'Or perhaps, in extreme cases, a skull and crossbones: robbery and extortion as well as poisoning. For these malefactors are the true sinners. They, and the criminal accomplices who swallow their wicked handiwork without a murmur. These accessories after the fact are guilty of a far greater sin than gluttony.' Mr Vortigern's voice had assumed a sepulchral note. 'I refer to Despair.

'Surely it is not casuistry to say that neglect of the fruits of the earth is doubting divine providence? Why do sturgeons swim in the Volga? Why do trout glitter and dart, what makes oysters assemble at Colchester and plovers lay their forbidden eggs? Why do turtles doze in the Seychelles and crustaceans change their carapaces and mushrooms rise from their dunghills and truffles lead sunless lives in Périgord and grouse dwell in the Pictish mists? Why do strawberries ripen and why do vine tendrils grow in those suggestive corkscrews? Why is the snail on the thorn? Is it to test us or is it a kindly providence at work? But the Fathers have spoken. It's no good trying to shift the blame or to say that sin lies only in excess. How can one eat caviar in moderation? There is another peculiar thing about gluttony: its physical penalties may be the heaviest, but it is the sin that leaves us with the lightest deposit of guilt. One feels like St Augustine – of Hippo, not Canterbury – postponing his reformation. 'Give me frugality and sobriety, Oh Lord,' one might paraphrase him, 'but not yet.' *Sed noli modo!* But it's no good. Cerberus and the hailstones are waiting.' Big Ben chimed its preliminary tune and began to toll the hour.

'There,' Mr Vortigern said, 'is the note of doom. I must go. . . . The time for emendation of life grows shorter. And the time for further backsliding too. . . . *Sed noli modo! Sed noli modo!*' His voice had regained its wonted buoyancy and his eyes were akindle, 'Are you free this evening? Capital. Come to me at eight o'clock. Don't be late. I won't tell you what we are going to have, but I think you will like it. The condemned men will eat a hearty dinner.'

SLOTH

SLOTH

Evelyn Waugh

THE word 'Sloth' is seldom on modern lips. When used, it is a mildly facetious variant of 'indolence', and indolence, surely, so far from being a deadly sin, is one of the most amiable of weaknesses. Most of the world's troubles seem to come from people who are too busy. If only politicians and scientists were lazier, how much happier we should all be. The lazy man is preserved from the commission of almost all the nastier crimes, and many of the motives which make us sacrifice to toil the innocent enjoyment of leisure, are among the most ignoble – pride, avarice, emulation, vainglory and the appetite for power over others. How then has Sloth found a place with its six odious companions as one of the Mortal Sins?

Theologians are the least rhetorical of writers. Their vocabulary is elaborate and precise, and when they condemn an act as a mortal sin they are not merely expressing disapproval in a striking phrase. They mean something specific and appalling; an outrage against the divine order committed with full knowledge and consent which, if unrepented before death, consigns the doer to eternal loss of salvation. Prelates and preachers may be found who use the words irresponsibly. One sometimes sees proclamations in which the faithful are exhorted to vote in an election or refrain from an entertainment 'under pain of mortal sin'. Moral theologians give little support to such utterances. Indeed many speculate that, the sanctions being so awful and the conditions so stringent, very few mortal sins have ever been committed. We only know that Hell is there for those who deliberately choose it. Shall we go there for lying too long in the bath or postponing our letters of congratulation or condolence? Obviously not. What then is this Sloth which can merit the extremity of divine punishment?

St Thomas's answer is both comforting and surprising: *tristitia de bono spirituali*, sadness in the face of spiritual good. Man is made for joy in the love of God, a love which he expresses in service. If he deliberately turns away from that joy, he is denying the purpose of his existence. The malice of Sloth lies not merely in the neglect of duty (though that can be a symptom of it) but in the refusal of joy. It is allied to despair.

There is a well-known pathological condition of religious melancholy in which the sufferer believes himself to be eternally damned through no particular fault of his own but by the ineluctable whim of the Almighty. In recent years, with the waning of Calvinist eloquence, this aberration seems to have tended to shed its religious trappings, but there are recognizable traces of it in some of the utterances of the 'beatniks'. Despair of this kind is not Sloth. Sloth is the condition in which a man is fully aware of the proper means of his salvation and refuses to take them because the whole apparatus of salvation fills him with tedium and disgust.

It is, one might suppose, a rare condition most often found among those who have dedicated themselves to a specifically religious vocation for which they find themselves unworthy, and not the prime temptation of men living in the world. Sixty years ago it would have been pedantic to treat of it in a secular journal, but, curiously enough, in this generation the man of Sloth, in all his full theological implications, has become one of the stock figures of stage and novel. The protagonists of these popular spiritual dramas, French, English, American, sometimes priests, are spoken of as having 'lost their Faith' as though Faith were an extraneous possession, like an umbrella, which can be inadvertently left behind in a railway-carriage; but in fact their predicament is quite different from that of their unhappy great-grandfathers who, confronted with plausible arguments that the universe took longer than six days in the making, decided that the whole foundation of their religion was spurious. These new apostates do not wrestle with historical and philosophic doubts; they simply lapse into 'sadness in the face of spiritual good'.

The plainest representation of this depth of Sloth, and the one likely to be freshest in the reader's memory, is Querry, the central character of Mr Graham Greene's recent novel, *A Burnt-Out Case*. He is an eminent architect who, like the less well-known writer, Morin, created by the same richly gifted writer, is sickened by the applause of admirers who persist in attributing his achievements to a love of God he has ceased to exercise. Love of his fellow men also dies in him. Eaten by apathy, self-pity and the sense of futility he tries to escape to the most remote refuge in central Africa where there happens to be a leper settlement. Here he dies a ludicrous death. The only change in him has been a twinge of affection for a servant and, at the instigation of an atheist doctor, an interest in the erection of some new sheds.

The author's intention, as in most of his later books, is obscure. Does he mean us to recognize in these feeble stirrings of humanity an act of the will which a theologian would recognize as contrition? We must not impute damnation to a human soul. With fictitious characters we are free to speculate. I should say that

on the facts given us by Mr Greene, Querry was guilty
and in Hell. He is one of a rather large company of
modern fictitious characters. The fact that they have so
captivated the artists and the public of the day suggests
that the problem is not so recondite as might have been
supposed. It must not be thought I am accusing Mr
Greene of Sloth. Artists often express vicarious experiences (most erotic writing is the work of the impotent). It would be impossible for a man who was
really guilty of Sloth to write about it, for he would be
incapable of the intense work required to produce a
novel like *A Burnt-Out Case*.

So much for the Sloth of the theologian, technically
dubbed *accidia (or acedia)*. There is no true classical term
for this state, not because it was unknown to the
ancients, but because it was too commonplace to require
identification. The last centuries of European paganism
before the revelation of Christian joy were sunk deep in
accidia. Now that paganism is returning we see the
symptoms again. Can we accuse our listless and torpid
contemporaries of Sloth in the sense defined above? I
think not, because the great majority have been de-
prived by the State of religious instruction. The phrase
'spiritual good' is totally foreign to them, and they lack
the full knowledge of its nature which is an essential
element in the commission of mortal sin.

There are, however, very near parallels, especially
in those whose calling has a superficial resemblance to
monastic life, the armed services. These men accept
higher standards of obedience than civilians and are
expected on occasions to make greater sacrifices.
'Browned-off' and 'bloody-minded' troops present a
type of Sloth. I have seen soldiers in defeat who could

not be accused of laziness. They were making strenuous exertions to get away from the enemy. Nor were they impelled by fear. They had simply become bored by the mismanagement of the battle and indifferent to its outcome. There were ill-found camps and stations in the war where men refused to take the actions which would have alleviated their own condition, but instead luxuriated in apathy and resentment. There was a sense of abandonment there which, though it was not recognized as such, was theological in essence; instead it found expression in complaints, just or unjust, against the higher command and the politicians.

It was suggested above that we were not putting ourselves in danger of Hell by indolence but, just as he is a poor soldier whose sole aim is to escape detention, so he is a poor Christian whose sole aim is to escape Hell. Besides *accidia* there is *pigritia*, plain slackness, which is a deflexion from, if not an outrage against, the divine order. This increasingly is a national characteristic, so closely allied to our national virtues of magnanimity and good temper as to be at times barely distinguishable from them. It is strange, in an age when the conscience is directed so constantly to social aims, that this vice so largely escapes censure, for if, as has been said, the personal motives of industry may be base, the consequences of idleness on society are conspicuously deleterious.

It is a fault about which we are particularly liable to self-deception. Almost all the men and women in England proclaim themselves to be busy. They have 'no time' to read or cook or take notice of the ceaseless process of spoliation of their island or even to dress decorously, while in their offices and workshops they do less and less, in quality and quantity, for ever larger wages with which to pay larger taxes for services that diminish in quantity and quality. We have voted for a Welfare State but are everywhere frustrated because we are too lazy to man the services; too few school teachers, too few hospital nurses, too few prison warders. That way lies national disaster; but the subject of this essay is moral, not political. There is something unattractive about those who gaze out of their windows for long periods studying the idleness of the navvies 'at work' outside. Let me speak of my own trade.

Since I first set up as a writer nearly thirty-five years ago I have witnessed a lamentable decline of power in all the processes of literature. The period between the delivery of a manuscript to the publishers and its appearance for sale as a book is now about three times what it was in my youth, as also is the period between ordering a book from a shop in the provinces and receiving it. The standards of printing have deteriorated. Compositors, equipped with mechanical devices unknown to their illustrious predecessors, are ruthless in setting up gibberish and preserving it against proof-corrections.

But it ill becomes authors to complain of the mechanics. We are ourselves in a situation peculiarly apt for self-deception, for there is no one except ourselves who can accuse us of idleness. The actual process of writing is laborious and irksome. We sit at our desks for, say, two hours and emerge with a thousand deathless words. But if we sit at our windows smoking, observing the birds, who is to say that we are not deep in aesthetic rumination? If we lounge in a foreign café, who is to say we are not 'collecting material'? Not the Commissioners of Income Tax.

You must know us by our works. How many of us display the 'hard gem-like flame' with which, for example, Max Beerbohm in his day illuminated even the columns of the *Daily Mail*? How many resolve that nothing shall leave the workshop which is not as perfectly finished as our talents allow? How many have simply given up the effort to plan and complete and adorn a work of art? Endowed with the most splendid language in the world, most of the young writers seem intent to debase and impoverish it.

Their elders do not set them a high example. If one considers the list of those who, twenty years ago, would have been expected to be now at the height of their powers, one finds a pitiably small band of survivors and those mainly men and women of the previous decade. The rest concern themselves with appearing on television, collaborating in film-scripts, and attending congresses where they call attention to the lack of prestige they are accorded. Of the hard, long work of actually writing books, most have despaired. How many reviewers, even in the respectable papers, read the book sent them with close enough attention to retail their plots or arguments without mistakes of pure laziness?

It may be noted that in the arts profusion, as much as sterility, may be evidence of laziness. Those huge novels from North America are not the product of diligence; hard labour would refine and clarify them. Some writers, it is said, leave this to their publishers, presenting them with trunk-loads of typescript from which a précis is made in the office. This is not a common trouble in this country. Here we suffer rather from the imposture of writers who produce their rough note and sketches as finished work and pretend to a unity in what are mere scraps of articles and lectures.

These are some of the evidence of Sloth in a single trade in a country where the vice is widely prevalent. They may seem of minor importance in the history of national decline but they are symptomatic of the whole disease, and literature was formerly the one art in which we could claim equality with (if not superiority to) the rest of the civilized world. Sloth is not such an innocent weakness as at first glance it appeared.

It is easy to find explanations of modern laziness. All the 'glittering prizes' of success have lately become tarnished. The company in the room at the top has lost the art of pleasing. But Sloth is not primarily the temptation of the young. Medical science has oppressed us with a new huge burden of longevity. It is in that last undesired decade, when passion is cold, appetites feeble, curiosity dulled, and experience has begotten cynicism, that *accidia* lies in wait as the final temptation to destruction. That is the time which is given a man to 'make his soul'. For few of us the hero's and martyr's privilege of a few clear days ending on the scaffold; instead an attenuated, bemused drifting into eternity. Death has not lost its terror in the new clinical arctic twilight. In this state we shall have to face the last deadly assault of the devil. It is then, perhaps, that we shall be able to resist only by the spiritual strength we have husbanded in youth.

LUST

LUST

Christopher Sykes

THE recent permission to describe erotic activity with the aid of the bluntest words in our
language (and in detail if so desired), does
not make the subject of Lust any easier to
deal with. In fact it makes it harder, since
most of these admired words are derisory, and the
movement to enlarge their currency weakens useful
conventions. I shall stick to the conventions neverthe-
less, opening in the style of the old-fashioned sermon,
with an intercession: 'May I resist the awful temptation
of hypocrisy and coyness.'

These temptations are not imaginary, nor confined to
prim souls. Of the seven deadly sins, Lust is the only
one about which all mankind (with very few exceptions)
knows something from experience. People own to this
awkward fact in general, but not in particular. Even in
an age which prides itself on being 'outspoken', people
usually remain careful to avoid any suggestion that they
themselves are prone to unlawful passions, or to the
extravaganza which goes with erotic feeling. Hence a
great measure of falsification in most writing and talk
on the subject, even in the most advanced society. But to
say, 'Lust is a vice I cannot understand' would be to over-
do it; it would not wash in any society at all. Hence the
flight from hypocrisy to coyness. All men are potentially
lustful, and a huge proportion are so in practice.

This raises the great question. If the vice, or the
instinct to the vice, is so universal, ought it to be condemned as a vice at all? Ought it even to be thought of
as wrong in any way, let alone as constituting a deadly
wrong?

So far as I know, the classic argument against the
condemnation of Lust is twofold, coming on the one

hand from people who regard religious prohibitions as part of an outworn phase of the human spirit, and on the other from people who respect and adhere to religion but question the balance of its teaching.

The first argument proceeds roughly as follows: Lust can be avoided only by an unnaturally powerful act of will. The fact that this act of will is against inclination inevitably results in harmful psychological strain and, as often as not, in a search for animal satisfactions outside the regions of sex, for example in aggressiveness or a brutal use of power; in activities which are far more harmful than the imagined wrongs of incontinence.

Furthermore, it is argued, to see wrong in sexual freedom is to see wrong in the order of nature, is to deny the beauty of the creation, and therefore, if you believe in God, is to deny the Creator's goodness and perfection. It is a blasphemy against life.

The second argument, while accepting the religious prohibition in general, objects to the enormous prominence given in Church teaching to Lust. As in the previous argument, the great demand made upon the will is blamed as excessive. It is objected that a person who succeeds in the effort of leading a chaste life, may often, except in circumstances of rare felicity, use up all moral energy in so doing. He or she will have none left for 'the first and great commandment', or for loving one's neighbour as oneself. Hence the by no means rare phenomenon of the upright churchgoer with an unblemished name and a heart of flint. Could anyone be remoter from the teaching of the New Testament? The moral teaching of Christianity is not adjured, according to this line of argument, but the heavy stress on the wickedness of erotic misconduct is held to be mistaken.

Such are the two most usual arguments against the prohibition. What are the arguments on the other side?

The usual one against sexual freedom is that such a proposal both underrates and exaggerates the importance of the erotic instincts. To take the exaggeration first: the belief that sex is the mainspring of human activity, and must therefore not be bent too much by the will; this commonly accepted notion, based on vulgarizations of modern psychological theory, is contested on the grounds that it is not supported by ordinary evidence. Though it is not a thing much mentioned in the papers, large numbers of people, probably the majority, appear content with sexual activity within the limits of the law. Total abstinence from sex, practised, with no harmful effect, by well-adjusted people, is by no means uncommon: scandals involving unmarried clergy or nuns are rare events.

The belief that continence provokes extra-sexual misconduct does not rest on any self-evident truth. With exceptions, criminals, both of the law-abiding and law-breaking kind, are not remarkable for chastity. There is no reason at all to suppose that sexual repression is a main cause of crime. Equally there is no reason to suppose that sexual liberation leads to an earthly paradise whose inhabitants lose all cruel impulse and dwell together in peace and bliss. The few societies, such as the Scandinavian or Japanese, which may be described as sexually free (by usual standards) do not seem to have automatically solved the riddles of human happiness and right behaviour. The evidence is that sexual freedom either has no improving effect, or causes at least as many problems as it solves.

It is here that the argument against underrating

sexual instinct comes in. This argument is simple, more ancient than history, and usually expressed in theological terms. To use profane terms, it may roughly be expressed as follows: man depends, for the bare maintenance of his human status, on the orderly and partial inhibition of the numerous passions which he shares with the animals. He naturally rebels against inhibition, as a tethered animal does, but this rebellious passion must also be inhibited along with the rest. Total inhibition must never be compelled, but to reject the partial inhibitions of sacred or profane law is to reject far more than the freedom-marchers guess, for the whole idea of inhibition involves the immense question whether man is merely another animal or something more. The circumstances of civilized life today offer new material for this line of argument with reference to Lust.

In most times and places the practice of Lust is regarded as a masculine preserve from which women are excluded on pain of severe and sometimes frightful punishments. But now, with female emancipation, this kind of sex-inequality, though still largely accepted, becomes increasingly difficult to maintain. The sauce for the gander can now be claimed by the goose, and often is. A noted French authoress has taken the matter to its logical conclusion and advocates officially licensed brothels for the use of female clients. Without such institutions, she asserts, sex-equality is a sham. Her proposal is likely to shock many people who regard themselves as unshockable, and perhaps one reason is that it forcibly brings out the main argument in favour of anti-lust legislation, and the more alarming implications of the pro-lust agitation.

For, of course, the whole idea that men and women are sexually on equal terms is ridiculous. This is not seriously disputed, though it is often overlooked that as a result of sexual inequality of function, there is a corresponding inequality in the means of sexual satisfaction. For many men, sexual congress in love completely suffices, but, as has been pointed out by authorities deserving respect, this is not so generally the case with women. Normally they achieve full sexual satisfaction through motherhood and nursing as well as through congress. (The emotion of fatherhood, though sexual, is sensually unconnected with physical sex-experience.)

If monogamy is considered too harsh a condition for men and women, if both sexes have equal rights, then it would seem from the foregoing that the correct thing to aim for is a large bastard population. This might result in many unpredictable social evils, including chronic and fanatical class conflict between the legitimately and illegitimately born. The final result might well be the complete abolition of marriage and the family background to life. Though extreme, this ultimate development is not impossible. Marriage gets a bad Press all round today, and the fact that by British revenue arrangements it is subject to penal taxation raises no protest from thinkers, politicians, the electorate, or the Churches. In many of the most civilized parts of the world it is an enfeebled institution.

This is, of course, to speak of monogamous marriage as if it were the only known kind. Legalized polygamy, including polyandry, has been and is practised successfully in many parts of the world. This is encouraging, is it not? Why not try it here? I am not learned enough to range a host of authorities for or against the polygamous

system, but it seems incontestable that although polygamy has operated successfully for long periods, it
is in reality a short-term solution. It seems to be an
acceptable way of life for people in a state of civilization
cruder than our own. In Islamic countries, where male
polygamy remains legal, it has for long been rejected
by the more educated, and this is not just due to the
monogamous influence of Europe.

One is tempted to say that Islamic polygamy de-
pended on an enslaved female population, but I think
that this is in some part a popular fallacy. Eastern
women, especially in tribal areas, were never the enslaved creatures of European fancy, and the enslave-
ment-theory can hardly be true of polyandry in the few
areas where it is practised. It is certainly true, however,
that educated and emancipated women make harem life
impossible, and it seems safe to say that most well-
educated men of virile temperament would not find the
discipline of polyandry agreeable.

The evidence is that if we agree to travel along the
road of civilized progress, there comes a moment when
we have to say goodbye to the consolations of multiple
marriage. In its place we can put frequent divorce, a
cause of unhappy childhood everywhere, and a frequent
cause of child-beggary in poor countries where divorce
is easy. But there seems to be no other possible com-
promise between monogamy and a measure of freedom
that would transform, and probably destroy, our fragile
civilization.

Against the numerous but less vocal rebels who
accept Christian teaching in the main, but question the
extreme Church condemnation of Lust, the argument is
necessarily less general. Clergymen point out that the

compassion of Jesus Christ to unchaste sinners involved
no commiseration of inchastity; that the famous utter-
ance, 'Her sins are forgiven her for she has loved much',
refers to sacred love and not, as is often believed, to
profane love, and that Christ's positive teaching on
chastity is extremely severe, as in His prohibition
against lustful ideas regardless of action, and in the
ideal of those who renounce all sexual pleasure 'for the
Kingdom of Heaven's sake'. In fact, moralists may
conclude, the supposed gospel leniency to inchastity is
conveniently imagined.

Is it? In part, perhaps, but the extraordinary fact
remains that Jesus Christ not only met but made friends
with harlots, and is only once recorded to have spoken
a harsh word to a loose-liver, the woman of Samaria,
and then in the course of a courteous dialogue which
resulted in instant conversion. He told no parable on
the subject of chastity (the foolish virgins were virgins),
and His harshest denunciation of inchastity is mild
compared to what He had to say on the subject of
hypocrisy, hardness of heart, and the parade of 'respectability' by the spiritually vain. Why does the
Church not put the stress here rather than on 'sins of
the flesh'? Why not call hypocrisy deadly rather than
Lust?

If I were a clergyman, I should not enjoy countering
that undoubtedly strong argument. But if I were a
clergyman, and had to somehow, I should point to a
certain misunderstanding about the seven deadly sins.
They were originally called 'capital sins', and the meaning, as I understand it, is not that they are more ghastly
than any others, but that indulgence in them involves
the sinner in many other sins besides; each one is the

'capital', so to speak of a whole territory of mischief and wrongdoing. In the case of Lust, it may be argued, if the compassion of Jesus Christ is translated into terms of tolerance, the primrose path thereby opened must lead first to an increase of such horrors as brothel-slavery, and ultimately to that deathly state of animal degradation that moralists foresee from the total sex freedom advocated by certain of the non-religious.

So far I have referred to familiar arguments on both sides, but of recent years a new and disturbing opposition to traditional morals has arisen. This comes from a school of ideas which has been described as a new romanticism. Followers of this movement see delusion in every human pretension, and their culture is Anti-Art.

I believe that the school is still too unformed to be indicated with precision, but the answer of this vanguard to the prohibitors is not in much doubt and would go roughly as follows:

'*What you say against lust has not the slightest force, because it originates in gigantic lies: in postulating that the moral sense is rational, that there is such a thing as reason, that individual men have some non-animal property or other – call it 'soul' – ugh! – or that the collective spirit of Man, which the less orthodox prefer to these individual 'souls' of yours, is inherently superior to the Collective Spirit of Pigs, Slugs, Trees, or Cabbages, if one likes to imagine anything so blatantly non-existent as a Spirit of any kind at all!*

'*Man the Paragon is an invention of our forefathers' vanity. You invite a choice between Ape and Angel. Apes for ever! What's wrong with them? Plenty, but at*

*least they exist, and a regular ape is worth a thousand
disguised apes trying to look like non-existent angels.
And regular apes, as opposed to your fancy-dress variety,
see nothing wrong in lust, if only for the very good
reason that they have no wish to be "human beings".
Man is obsolete.'*

The last sentence is a quotation. I think I see the
counter-argument.

The weakness of this new school of no-humanism,
no-morality, no-reason, no-art, is surely that its argument depends on an appeal to those moral values which
it rejects, notably the love of truth. If I am not mistaken,
its followers are in the same philosophical jam as
plagues the behaviourists, of whom Aldous Huxley
wisely remarked that if their belief in behaviourism is
sound, then there is no reason to attach importance to
anything a behaviourist may say.

In these reflections I have not given much of my own
view. Haven't I got one? All the world loves a lover.
Don't you? Of course I do. I have known many people
whom you could call lovers and whom I have loved.
By no stretch of the imagination can I feel personally
condemnatory on the subject. All the same, I will go
with the moralists in not loving Don Juan. He seems to
me merely the inverse of the flinty-hearted Pharisee:
all the mental and moral energy used up in the strenuous play of seduction.

In the few of the species whom I have known, I
notice one characteristic in common: an ineradicable
vulgarity, an essential commonness of mind. Off their
beat they are dull dogs. I suppose the coarseness of
character in these people provides striking evidence

that the notion of the 'capital' sin commanding subsidiaries has great psychological depth. Promiscuous love necessitates hypocrisy. To play the part of Don Juan you need to be word-perfect in that of Tartuffe as well.

ANGER

ANGER

W. H. Auden

L IKE all the sins except pride, anger is a perversion, caused by pride, of something in our nature which in itself is innocent, necessary to our existence and good. Thus, while everyone is proud in the same way, each of us is angry or lustful or envious in his own way.

Natural, or innocent, anger is the necessary reaction of a creature when its survival is threatened by the attack of another creature and it cannot save itself (or its offspring) by flight. Such anger, accompanied by physiological changes, like increased secretion of adrenalin, inhibits fear so that the attacked creature is able to resist the threat to its extinction. In the case of young creatures that are not yet capable of looking after themselves, anger is a necessary emotion when their needs are neglected: a hungry baby does right to scream. Natural anger is a reflex reaction, not a voluntary one; it is a response to a real situation of threat and danger, and as soon as the threat is removed, the anger subsides. No animal lets the sun go down upon its wrath. Moreover, Lorentz has shown that, in fights between the social animals, when, by adopting a submissive posture, the weaker puts itself at the mercy of the stronger, this inhibits further aggression by the latter.

Anger, even when it is sinful, has one virtue; it overcomes sloth. Anybody, like a schoolmaster, a stage director or an orchestral conductor, whose business it is to teach others to do something, knows that, on occasions, the quickest – perhaps the only – way to get those under him to do their best is to make them angry.

Anger as a sin is either futile (the situation in which one finds oneself cannot or should not be changed, but must be accepted) or unnecessary (the situation could be mastered as well or better without it). Man is potentially capable of the sin of anger because he is endowed with memory – the experience of an event persists – and with the faculty of symbolization (to him, no object or event is simply itself). He becomes actually guilty of anger because he is first of all guilty of the sin of pride, of which anger is one of many possible manifestations.

Because every human being sees the world from a unique perspective, he can, and does, choose to regard himself as its centre. The sin of anger is one of our reactions to any threat, not to our existence, but to our fancy that our existence is more important than the existence of anybody or anything else. None of us wishes to be omnipotent, because the desires of each are limited. We are glad that other things and people exist with their own ways of behaving – life would be very dull if they didn't – so long as they do not thwart our own. Similarly, we do not want others to conform with our wishes because they must – life would be very lonely if they did – but because they choose to; we want DEVOTED slaves.

The British middle-class culture in which I grew up strongly discouraged overt physical expression of anger; it was far more permissive, for example, towards gluttony, lust and avarice. In consequence, I cannot now remember 'losing' my temper so that I was beside myself and hardly knew what I was doing. Since childhood, at least, I have never physically assaulted anyone, thrown things or chewed the carpet. (I do, now and again, slam doors.) Nor have I often seen other people do these things. In considering anger, therefore, most of my facts are derived from introspection and may not be valid for others, or from literature, in which truth has to be subordinated to dramatic effect. No fits of temper in real life are quite as interesting as those of Lear, Coriolanus or Timon.

In my own case – I must leave the psychological explanation to professionals – my anger is more easily aroused by things and impersonal events than by other people. I don't, I believe, really expect others to do what I wish and am seldom angry when they don't; on the other hand I do expect God or Fate to oblige me. I do not mind losing at cards if the other players are more skilful than I, but, if I cannot help losing because I have been dealt a poor hand, I get furious. If traffic lights fail to change obligingly to red when I wish to cross the road, I am angry; if I enter a restaurant and it is crowded, I am angry. My anger, that is to say, is most easily aroused by a situation which is (a) not to my liking, (b) one I know I cannot change, and (c) one for which I can hold no human individual responsible.

Change of Nature

This last condition is the most decisive. I like others to be on time and hate to be kept waiting, but if someone deliberately keeps me waiting because, say, he is annoyed with me or wishes to impress me with his importance, I am far less angry than I am if I know him to be unpunctual by nature. In the first case, I feel I must be partly responsible – if I had behaved otherwise in the past, he would not have kept me waiting; and I feel hopeful – perhaps I can act in the future in such a way that our relationship will change and he will be punctual next time. In the second case, I know that it is in his nature to be late for others, irrespective of their relationship, so that, in order to be on time, he would have to become another person.

My fantastic expectation that fate will do as I wish goes so far that my immediate reaction to an unexpected event, even a pleasant surprise, is anger.

Among the British middle class, repressed physical violence found its permitted substitute in verbal aggression, and the more physically pacific the cultural sub-group (academic and clerical circles, for instance), the more savage the tongue – one thinks of the families in Miss Compton-Burnett's novels, or of Professor Housman jotting down deadly remarks for future use.

Compared with physical aggression, verbal aggression has one virtue; it does not require the presence of its victim. To say nasty things about someone behind his back is at least preferable to saying them to his face. On the other hand, for intelligent and talented persons, it has two great moral dangers. First, verbal malice, if witty, wins the speaker social approval. (Why is it that kind remarks are very seldom as funny as unkind?) Secondly, since, in verbal malice, the ill-will of the heart is associated with the innocent play of the imagination, a malicious person can forget that he feels ill-will in a way that a physically aggressive person cannot. His audience, however, is not so easily deceived. Two people may make almost the same remark; one, we feel immediately, is being only playful, the other has a compulsive wish to denigrate others.

Self-importance

Simone Weil has described how, when she was suffering from acute migraine, she felt a desire to strike others on the same spot where she felt the pain herself. Most acts of cruelty, surely, are of this kind. We wish to make others suffer because we are impotent to relieve our own sufferings (which need not, of course, be physical). Any threat to our self-importance is enough to create a lifelong resentment, and most of us, probably, cherish a great deal more resentment than we are normally aware of. I like to fancy myself as a kind-hearted person who hates cruelty. And why shouldn't I be kind? I was loved as a child, I have never suffered a serious injury either from another individual or from society, and I enjoy good health. Yet, now and again, I meet a man or a woman who arouses in me the desire to ill-treat them. They are always perfectly harmless people, physically unattractive (I can detect no element of sexual sadism in my feelings) and helpless. It is, I realize with shame, their helplessness which excites my ill-will. Here is someone who, whatever I did to him or her, would not fight back, an ideal victim, therefore, upon whom to vent all my resentments, real or imagined, against life.

If it were really possible for suffering to be transferred like a coin from one person to another, there might be circumstances in which it was morally permissible; and if, however mistakenly, we believed that it was possible, acts of cruelty might occasionally be excusable. The proof that we do not believe such a transfer to be possible is that, when we attempt it, we are unsatisfied unless the suffering we inflict upon others is at least a little greater than the suffering that has been inflicted upon ourselves.

The transferability-of-suffering fallacy underlies the doctrine of retributive punishment, and there is so little evidence that the threat of punishment – the threat of public exposure is another matter – is an effective deterrent to crime, or that its infliction – self-inflicted penance is again another matter – has a reformatory effect, that it is impossible to take any other theory of punishment seriously. By punishment, I mean, of course, the deliberate infliction of physical or mental suffering beyond what the safety of others requires. There will probably always be persons who, whether they like it or not, have to be quarantined, some, perhaps, for the rest of their lives.

'Righteous Anger'

The anger felt by the authorities which makes them eager to punish is of the same discreditable kind which one can sometimes observe among parents and dog-owners, an anger at the lack of respect for his betters which the criminal has shown by daring to commit his crime. His real offence in the eyes of the authorities is not that he has done something wrong but that he has done something which THEY have forbidden.

'Righteous anger' is a dubious term. Does it mean anything more than that there are occasions when the sin of anger is a lesser evil than cowardice or sloth? I know that a certain state of affairs or the behaviour of a certain person is morally evil and I know what should be done to put an end to it; but, without getting angry, I cannot summon up the energy and the courage to take action.

Righteous anger can effectively resist and destroy evil, but the more one relies upon it as a source of energy, the less energy and attention one can give to the good which is to replace the evil once it has been removed.

That is why, though there may have been some just wars, there has been no just peace. Nor is it only the vanquished who suffer; I have known more than one passionate anti-Nazi who went to pieces once Hitler had been destroyed. Without Hitler to hate, their lives had no *raison d'être*.

'One should hate the sin and love the sinner.' Is this possible? The evil actions which I might be said to hate are those which I cannot imagine myself committing. When I read of the deeds of a Hoess or an Eichmann, from whom I have not personally suffered, though I certainly do not love them, their minds are too unintelligible to hate. On the other hand, when I do something of which I am ashamed, I hate myself, not what I have done; if I had hated it, I should not have done it.

I wish the clergy today – I am thinking of the Anglican Church because She is the one I know best – would not avoid, as they seem to, explaining to us what the Church means by Hell and the Wrath of God. The public is left with the impression, either that She no longer believes in them or that She holds a doctrine which is a moral monstrosity no decent person could believe.

Theological definitions are necessarily analogical, but it is singularly unfortunate that the analogies for Hell which the Church has used in the past should have been drawn from Criminal Law. Criminal laws are imposed laws – they come into being because some people are not what they should be, and the purpose of the law is to compel them by force and fear to behave. A law can always be broken and it is ineffective unless the authorities have the power to detect and punish, and the resolution to act at once.

To think of God's laws as imposed leads to absurdities. Thus, the popular conception of what the Church means by Hell could not unfairly be described as follows. God is an omniscient policeman who is not only aware of every sin we have committed but also of every sin we are going to commit. But for seventy years or so He does nothing, but lets every human being commit any sin he chooses. Then, suddenly, He makes an arrest and, in the majority of cases, the sinner is sentenced to eternal torture.

Souls in Hell

Such a picture is not without its appeal; none of us likes to see his enemies, righteous or unrighteous, flourishing on earth like a green bay tree. But it cannot be called Christian. Some tender-minded souls have accepted the analogy but tried to give eternity a time limit: in the end, they say, the Devil and damned will be converted. But this is really no better. God created the world; He was not brought in later to make it a good one. If His love could ever be coercive and affect the human will without its co-operation, then a failure to exercise it from the first moment would make Him directly responsible for all the evil and suffering in the world.

If God created the world, then the laws of the spiritual life are as much laws of our nature as the laws of physics and physiology, which we can defy but not break. If I jump out of the window or drink too much I cannot be said to break the law of gravity or a biochemical law, nor can I speak of my broken leg or my hangover as a punishment inflicted by an angry Nature. As Wittgenstein said: 'Ethics does not treat of the world. Ethics must be a condition of the world like logic.' To speak of the Wrath of God cannot mean that God is Himself angry. It is the unpleasant experience of a creature, created to love and be happy, when he defies the laws of his spiritual nature. To believe in Hell as a possibility is to believe that God cannot or will not ever compel us to love and be happy. The analogy which occurs to me is with neurosis. (This, of course, is misleading too because, in these days, many people imagine that, if they can call their behaviour neurotic, they have no moral responsibility for it). A neurotic, an alcoholic, let us say, is not happy; on the contrary, he suffers terribly, yet no one can relieve his suffering without his consent and this he so often withholds. He insists on suffering because his ego cannot bear the pain of facing reality and the diminution of self-importance which a cure would involve.

If there are any souls in Hell, it is not because they have been sent there, but because Hell is where they insist upon being.